The Danse Macabre

PRINTED BY GUYOT MARCHANT, 1485

TRANSLATED BY

David A. Fein

ARIZONA CENTER FOR MEDIEVAL

ACMRS

AND RENAISSANCE STUDIES

Tempe, Arizona
2013

Published by ACMRS (Arizona Center for Medieval and Renaissance Studies),
Tempe, Arizona.
©2013 Arizona Board of Regents for Arizona State University.
All Rights Reserved.

Library of Congress Cataloging-in-Publication Data

Danse macabre des femmes. English
  The Danse Macabre (Printed by Guyot Marchant, 1485) / translated by David
A. Fein.
      pages cm. -- (Medieval and Renaissance Texts and Studies ; Volume 446)
(MRTS Texts for Teaching ; Volume 7)
  Includes bibliographical references and index.
  ISBN 978-0-86698-495-9 (acid-free paper)
1. Dance of Death. 2. Dialogues, French--Translations into English. 3. Wood-
engraving, French--15th century. 4. Death--Poetry. I. Marchant, Guy. II. Fein,
David A., translator. III. Title.
  PQ1561.D36E5 2013
  841'.1--dc23

                                                              2013036964

∞
This book is made to last. It is set in Adobe Caslon Pro,
smyth-sewn and printed on acid-free paper to library specifications.
Printed in the United States of America

TABLE OF CONTENTS

INTRODUCTION

Brief History of the *Danse Macabre*

Although one of the earliest visual representations of the *danse macabre*, appearing as paintings on the inner wall of the Parisian Cemetery of the Innocents in 1425, was destroyed over three centuries ago, a successful printer, Guyot Marchant, who specialized in scholarly Latin treatises, decided to publish a copy of the images and the accompanying inscription in 1485.[1] The little volume quickly sold out, and was succeeded by a series of subsequent editions. Although the contribution of Marchant's book to the spread of the *danse macabre* throughout Western Europe during the next few decades cannot be clearly delineated, the transformation of the murals into a portable version can only have accelerated the popularity of these images and their accompanying text.[2] Despite its importance as a cultural artifact, as a transformative vehicle facilitating the spread of the *danse*, and as a powerful articulation of the late medieval preoccupation with human mortality, Marchant's book remains relatively unknown to those unable to read it in the original. The present translation is intended to make the work accessible to a wider audience.

According to *Le Journal d'un bourgeois de Paris*, the fresco was actually begun in August of 1424 and completed around Lent of 1425:

> Item, l'an 1424, fut faite la Danse Macabre aux Innocents, et fut commencée environ le mois d'août et achevée au Carême ensuivant. (In the year 1424 the Danse Macabre was created in [the Cemetery of] the Innocents around the month of August and was completed by the following Lent.) (ed. Beaune, 220)

The painting consisted of individual panels, each depicting a confrontation between the living and the dead, representing various social stations, alternating between religious and secular figures, starting at the top of the hierarchy with pope and emperor and descending to a mendicant friar, a peasant, and finally

---

[1] P. Vaillant, "La danse macabre de 1485 et les fresques du charnier des Innocents (à Paris)," in *La Mort au Moyen Âge* (Strasbourg: Istra, 1977), 81–86.

[2] See J. Kowzam, "Dance of Death," in *Oxford Dictionary of the Middle Ages* [hereafter *ODMA*], 4 vols. (Oxford: Oxford University Press, 2010), 2:481.

a newborn child. Running beneath the paintings was a poem, providing a dialogue between the figures of each panel. The cemetery was cleared for building
purposes in the seventeenth century, and no remnants of the frescoes were pre-
served. The images and text of the cemetery's famous *danse macabre* are known
today mainly through Marchant's book.

The Cemetery of *Les Saints Innocents* was affiliated with a relatively poor
parish church, which shared the land with other local churches. Sophie Oosterwijk precisely situates the cemetery in Paris and also the location of the *danse
macabre* within the confines of the churchyard:

> The church was situated close to where Les Halles used to be, along the rue
> Saint-Denis from the north near to where it met the rue de la Ferronnerie,
> which was the extension of the rue Saint-Honoré, the major thoroughfare
> from the west . . . The mural was painted onto the south gallery wall of the
> 'charnier des Lingères' that ran alongside the rue de la Ferronnerie, and
> appears to have occupied eleven bays. ("Historical Context," 132–33)

Although the origin of the *danse macabre* remains somewhat nebulous, its resem-
blance to a popular medieval text, *le Dit des trois vifs et trois morts*, is widely rec-
ognized. The earliest version is a work by Baudoin de Condé, written around
1285. Several subsequent versions in French appear at the end of the thirteenth
and well into the fourteenth century. Versions in German, Latin, Italian, and
English also date from the fourteenth century. The confrontation between three
socially privileged young men and three corpses parallels the *danse macabre* with
its stark contemplation of human mortality. While the *danse macabre*, however,
depicts various figures at the moment of their death, those in *le Dit des trois vifs
et trois morts* receive an early warning of their eventual fate, and are urged to
reform their lives accordingly. A psalter from the fourteenth century (belong-
ing to Bonne de Luxembourg, and dating from approximately 1340) contains
an illustration inspired by the story. A sculptural representation of the scene was
created on the exterior of the chapel of Saint-Michel in 1408 by the order of the
Duke, Jean de Berry, but the relief no longer exists. A fourteenth-century fresco
in the Campo Santo of Pisa depicts a related scene in which a group of aristocratic men and women on horseback encounter several corpses, over which hov-
ers the figure of death, personified as a woman in a long dress with white hair
and batlike wings, holding a huge scythe.

The etymology of the term *macabre* is uncertain. It first appears in Jean
le Fèvre's *Respit de la mort* (1376): "Je fis de Macabre la danse." The term has
been connected to the *Chorea Machabaeorum*, the "dance of the Maccabees."
Another possible etymological connection is the Arabic *makabir*, meaning tomb
or cemetery. A painter by the name of Macabré, one of whose paintings may
have inspired Jean le Fèvre, has also been cited. While its etymology remains
somewhat obscure, the physical context of the artistic motif in the Cemetery of

the Innocents is fairly well known. By the fifteenth century the cemetery was filled to capacity, necessitating the evacuation of numerous graves in order to make room for new burials. The disinterred bones were relocated to the charnel houses that lined the inner perimeter. Thus, fifteenth-century viewers of the *danse macabre* frescoes would simultaneously have immediate visual access to the physical evidence of human mortality graphically illustrated by the paintings. François Villon refers directly to the charnel houses of the Innocents toward the end of the *Testament*: "Quand je considere ces testes / Entassées en ces charni-ers . . ." (ll. 1744–1745) [When I consider these heads, piled up in these charnel houses . . .]. As the largest and most important cemetery of fifteenth-century Paris, the Innocents, like other cemeteries of the period, hosted a variety of secular activities completely unrelated to its religious function, and was routinely chosen by itinerant merchants, beggars, prostitutes, and others as an advantageous site for their business.

The *danse macabre* is not a dance of death but a dance of the dead. Each living figure is paired with a dead counterpart whose appearance resembles a mummy more than a skeleton. The opposition between the living and dead, as depicted in the woodcuts of the *Danse Macabre*, operates on several levels. Perhaps the most obvious contrast relates to the clothing of the living and the virtual nakedness of the dead. While the former are always fully clothed, the latter, if clothed at all, wear nothing but a loose-fitting shroud. While the living identify their specific position in the social hierarchy by their manner of dress (and sometimes by the symbolic objects they carry), the figures of the dead, stripped to the flesh and sometimes even to the bone, remind their living counterparts of the superficiality and meaninglessness of the material and social distinctions that separate one class from another. The second level of opposition is based on their contrasting attitudes, i.e., the opposition between their actual bodily postures. Early in the work, for example, we see the cardinal and the king urged by two corpses to join in the dance. The living figures remain relatively immobile, the cardinal staring with alarm at the hand of the corpse on his sleeve, the king standing rigidly as he holds his scepter. The corpse between them, on the other hand, assumes a more flexible pose, raising one leg as he prepares to lead away the two unwilling subjects. We see the same contrast in the illustration depicting the bishop and the squire. Again, the posture of the two corpses, especially the one in the middle, suggests a certain naturalness and fluidity of movement, while that of the bishop and squire indicates immobility and even (in the case of the squire) a marked attitude of resistance. By raising one hand in a gesture of refusal, pointing his feet in the opposite direction from those of the corpse, and leaning slightly away from his "partner," the squire's body language expresses a futile attempt at escape.

Artistic Representations of the *Danse Macabre*

Although the woodcuts in Marchant's book can, at best, provide only a limited representation of the large images that adorned the interior wall of the Innocents, a few frescoes of the *danse macabre* motif, dating from roughly the same period, survive in varying conditions in France and other parts of Europe, including England, Germany, and Switzerland. The fresco of Kermaria-Nisquit (a small village in Brittany), dating from the second half of the fifteenth century, is comprised of forty-seven figures, some of which have been almost completely effaced, covering three walls of the chapel. The inscription largely replicates that of the Innocents. The Church of Saint Germain in La Ferté-Loupière (Burgundy) contains a mural representing the *danse macabre*, dating from the end of the fifteenth or early sixteenth century, covering approximately twenty-five meters of the north wall. The church of Meslay-le-Grenet, near Chartres, contains a fresco from approximately the same period. The Benedictine abbey of Chaise-Dieu in Auvergne houses one of the best-preserved representations of the *danse macabre*, painted between 1460 and 1470, measuring twenty-six meters in length, and starting three meters from the floor. The dimensions of the surviving frescoes suggest the size of the *danse macabre* appearing on the inner wall of the Innocents, dimensions that were clearly calculated to impress the observer, and which are, of course, left to the imagination of those who view them reduced to page-sized woodcuts in Marchant's book.

The Cemetery of the Innocents

The energy suggested by the dancing figures of the dead may be seen as a reflection of the active environment of the Innocents, promoting a variety of social and commercial interactions. Paul Binski reminds us that medieval cemeteries, and the Innocents in particular, were not always dominated by a sense of contemplation and tranquility:

> The cemetery was not an empty place, but throbbed with the noise of betrothals, meetings, commerce, bread-baking, and judicial processes in and around the church porch. The Innocents confronted one of the largest markets of medieval Paris. The Dance was a vigorous piece of taboo-breaking, connecting ritually purified spaces to the signs of fallen human nature in the world in all its worldliness. (*Medieval Death*, 155)

Binski explores further parallels between the *danse macabre* and its immediate context, focusing on various kinds of promiscuity suggested by the dance and the human remains by which it is framed:

The fact of its early occurrence at the Innocents, a charnel, is significant: structurally, the Dance shuffled the dead and the living, regardless of station, just as the charnel shuffled the bones of the greatest with those of the least. It is ironic that this most trenchant expression of promiscuity between the living and the dead should have occurred at a famous haunt of prostitutes. (157)

Memento Mori

The *danse macabre* motif is only one manifestation of the late medieval preoccupation with death and mortality that takes several prominent forms in the art and literature of the period. One of these is the *memento mori* ("Remember you will die").[3] This motif is principally associated with funeral art and architecture, represented in the figure of the *transi*, a partially decomposed corpse appearing on sculpted tombs in parts of northern Europe during the fifteenth century and later.[4] These "cadaver tombs" are normally comprised of two tiers, with the *gisant,* the effigy of the deceased lying in a recumbent position, on the upper level, and with the *transi,* in an advanced state of deterioration, occupying the lower level. Given the cost, the exceptional artistic skill required to produce one of these tombs, and the large amount of space required for its display (normally inside a church or chapel), this type of tomb was reserved for only the wealthiest patrons and those occupying the highest ranks of the social or religious hierarchy. The *memento mori* motif in funeral architecture, like the *danse macabre*, is clearly inscribed within a strong didactic tradition, reminding viewers of the fate that awaits them, and implicitly urging them to reflect on their spiritual state and on the divergent paths leading to salvation and damnation. (The *memento mori* motif continued to evolve as late as the nineteenth century, when it took the curious form of post-mortem photography, also known as memorial portraiture, in which the deceased were photographed in lifelike poses, sometimes in the company of one or more family members.)

Ars Moriendi

The *danse macabre* may also be connected to another important manifestation of the late medieval preoccupation with death, the *Ars moriendi.* There are two versions of this work dating from the first half of the fifteenth century, the *Tractatus artis bene moriendi*, written around 1415 by a Dominican friar at the behest of the Council of Constance, and an abbreviated version, printed around 1450.

---

[3] For the German version see F.G. Gentry, *"Memento mori,"* in *ODMA*, 3: 1122.
[4] See K. Cohen, *Metamorphosis of a Death Symbol: The Transi Tomb in the Late Middle Ages and the Renaissance* (Berkeley: University of California Press, 1973).

The work rapidly attained great popularity, and was eventually translated into French, Spanish, Catalan, English, German, and Dutch. It offers specific advice to those who find themselves on their deathbed, and also to those charged with caring for these dying patients—specific protocols to be followed, including pre-scribed words and gestures, strategies for resisting diabolic attempts to seize the soul of the dying person, and the actions, thoughts, and words that will lead to salvation during this critically dramatic moment of decision. One explanation for the work's popularity involves the high rate of mortality from the plagues that swept across Western Europe throughout the fifteenth century, and the conse-quent need for those attending the dying, whether operating in a clerical or lay capacity, to be acquainted with the Church's teachings and practices concerning the critical hours immediately preceding death. The *Ars moriendi* also reflects a shift in theological thinking during the late medieval period, orienting divine judgment away from a collective assessment taking place at the end of human history toward an individual encounter taking place at the moment of death.

The shorter version of the *Ars moriendi* essentially represents a reworking of the second chapter of the longer version, reflecting the conflict between the forces of good and evil as the moment of death approaches, with the fate of the dying person's soul hanging in the balance. The work is basically structured around five temptations that the forces of evil inflict upon the moribund victim, which are countered by five discourses of wisdom provided by the angelic presence pro-tecting the soul in question. This conflict is dramatized in the work's woodcuts that depict a human figure on the deathbed, with several small demonic figures, naked and grotesque, reaching toward the bed, while a group of angels and saints stand on the other side of the bed, sometimes making gestures of entreaty, sup-port, or compassion. Philippe Ariès, in *The Hour of Our Death*, describes the drama of the deathbed as depicted in the *Ars moriendi*:

> The bedroom, however, was to take on a new meaning in the iconogra-phy of death. . . . It became the arena in which the fate of the dying man was decided for the last time, in which his whole life and all his passions and attachments were called into question. . . . Supernatural beings have invaded the bedroom and are crowding around his bedside. On one side are the Trinity, the Virgin, and the whole court of heaven, and the guardian angel; on the other side, Satan and his monstrous army of demons. (108)

The *Ars moriendi* is more than a simple manual for those charged with care of the dying. The work is intended to validate the will of the dying, who have the power, under proper guidance and with the benefit of strong moral and spiritual support, to choose the path leading to redemption and salvation. Here the *Ars moriendi* complements the *danse macabre*. Both works (at least the later versions of the *Ars moriendi* translated from Latin into the vernacular) are destined for popu-lar reception. Both are chiefly concerned with moral decisions that bring about far-reaching consequences of momentous importance to the individual involved. They approach the moment of death, of course, from opposite sides, one concentrating on the moment immediately preceding death, and the other on the degradation of the human body after death, and on the finality of bad decisions that are driven by physical desires of every type for the gratification of that body.

The Dance

Jane H.M. Taylor, in her article "Que signifiait danse au quinzième siècle? Danser la Danse macabré," reminds us that medieval dances, by and large, fall into one of two major categories. Aristocratic dance is characterized by " . . . une esthétique linéaire: on recherchait la ligne longue et souple, on rejetait tout mouvement qui contreviendrait à la retenue raffinée des participants" (265). This is definitely not the dance we see depicted in the images of the *danse macabre*, in which the dancing dead assume exaggerated, mocking, contorted, and almost grotesque postures, strongly suggesting a form of dance associated with a lower social station: "La danse paysanne, par contre, supposait un certain défoulement: on recherchait une certaine angularité, et les danses, plus vives et plus grossières, étaient surtout sautées au lieu d'être marchées mesurément" (265). The dance itself, although it cannot be conclusively identified from the illustrations, seems consistent with various popular dances of the period based on lines of dancers—the *branle*, the *carole*, and the *farendole*, for example.[5] The *danse paysanne* often takes on a lewd and vulgar character, bordering on the obscene. Thus, the very postures of the dancing corpses serve to mock and insult the living, especially those of unusually high social station (pope, emperor, cardinal, etc.) who, under normal circumstances, would never have direct contact with anyone involved in such vulgar displays.

Theatrical Origins

The *danse macabre*, of course, is more than a mere dance. There is compelling evidence suggesting a number of important connections between the *danse macabre* and certain theatrical genres, and various versions of the *danse* were likely performed throughout the fifteenth century. It could also be argued with

---

[5] I would like to thank my former colleague, Carol Marsh, in the University of North Carolina at Greensboro School of Music, for providing background on popular dances of the period. See also T.J. McGee, "Dances and Dance Music," in *ODMA*, 2:481–82; and A. Espinosa, "Music and the Danse Macabre: A Survey," in *The Symbolism of Vanitas in the Arts, Literature, and Music*, ed. L. de Girolami-Cheney (Lewiston, NY: Mellen, 1992), 15–31.

some justification that the *danse* reflects important aspects of the farce. The deflation of pretension and ambition, swift reversals of fortune, the undercutting of social conventions meant to protect and maintain the status of certain privileged members of society—all of these hallmarks of the farce may be found in the illustrations of Marchant's *Danse Macabre*. The figures of the living in their stiff poses, often ornately costumed according to their social station, bewildered and perplexed by their sudden confrontation with death, and unable to fully comprehend their precarious situation, offer perfect targets for mockery. The farce, of course, generally empowers a socially inferior figure (a peasant, a woman, a fool) with the ability to dominate a more powerful character. In this reversal of the social norm, it is the "weaker" figures who end up controlling the action, manipulating their victims, choreographing the dance. The parallels with the *Danse Macabre* are obvious. The figures endowed with the most power—emperors, kings, popes, cardinals—as well as those possessing exceptional knowledge—astrologers, physicians, scholars—are all defeated by nothing more than a naked, grinning corpse.

The grouping of the figures and the somewhat exaggerated nature of their poses also suggest a theatrical tableau. Like the characters in a farce, the living figures often give the impression of caricatures. In the scene depicting the usurer, for example, we see a corpse insistently tugging on the arm of the moneylender, who is so preoccupied with his transaction that he does not even feel the fatal touch. Towards the end of the *Danse Macabre* we find an especially revealing woodcut, depicting this time two living figures (the clerk and the hermit) and three corpses. The corpses at either end of the line are preparing to escort their victims to their fate. The corpse between the clerk and the hermit, who has positioned himself in the exact center of the image, is pausing, however, to take a bow (or so it would appear). The posture of this particular figure is unlike that of any other to be found in the series, and the distinguishing aspect of this gesture, coupled with its appearance toward the end of the lengthy procession, strongly suggests the bow of an actor who has completed his performance.

Mirror Imagery

The *danse macabre* sets in relief, among a number of other important dichotomies, the universality and fragility of the human condition, on the one hand, and, on the other, the particular and somewhat idiosyncratic confrontation with death that marks the end of each individual life. As Ashby Kinch observes, the figures of the dead employ specific language appropriate to the social station or profession of their living counterparts:

> Death employs legal terminology to inveigh against the lawyer's immoral practices; the language of debt accounting to blast the usurer; and the

language of pastoral responsibility to accuse the bishop of failing to attend to his duties to his "sheep." Precise registers of language allow death to engage each individual in terms that are recognizable in his social life. ("The Danse Macabre," 180)

Kinch, like a number of other scholars commenting on the *danse macabre*, uses the term "death" when referring to the figures of the dead, and while it is true that the latter can be seen as a general personification of the former, the distinction is important. The power of the *danse macabre*, both in its visual and verbal manifestations, resides to some degree in a personalized encounter with death. Each man confronts not an abstract representation of death, but a corpse who demonstrates in graphic detail how he himself will eventually appear, who addresses him in a familiar language and mercilessly mocks the weaknesses of his living counterpart that he knows so well. It is the mirror-like aspect of the *danse macabre* that endows it with a certain intimate and haunting quality. The image of the mirror is explicitly presented in the prologue to Marchant's 1486 edition:

> En ce miroer chascun peut lire
> Quil lui convient ainsi danser
> Saige est celuy qui bien sy mire
> Le mort le vif fait avancer
> Tu vois les plus grans commancer
> Car il nest nul que mort ne fiere
> Cest piteuse chose y panser
> Tout est forgie dune matiere

[In this mirror each can read / That he will have to dance in this way. / Wise is he who observes himself in it correctly / The corpse makes the living one step forward. / You see those of highest station begin /For Death spares no one. / It is a subject of sad reflection / All men are made of the same matter.]

The poem is preceded in this edition by an explanatory note characterizing the work as a *miroer salutaire pour toutes gens*. The image of the mirror actually functions at multiple levels, and it is more complex than it initially appears. Beyond the obvious pairing of the living and the dead, the living figures also, to some extent, mirror each other. Despite significant differences in their attire, they repeat the same stiff postures of resistance, the same gestures of surprise and expressions of dismay. The skeletal partner of the living figure appearing in each scene reinforces the mirror-like character of the work. The text inscribed beneath each panel of the cemetery fresco serves as a verbal reflection of the visual image. The most important mirrored reflection, of course, is that of the observers, initially the fifteenth-century visitors to the Cemetery of the Innocents, who, with a little imagination, would find their own images reflected somewhere among the figures of the *danse macabre*.[6]

Verse Form

The text of the *Danse Macabre* takes the form of a versified dialogue between the figures of the living and the dead. The work is divided into eight-line stanzas, *huitains*, consisting of octosyllabic verse with the following rhyme scheme: ABABBCBC. This stanza type appears in many fifteenth-century works, including those by François Villon who uses the *huitain* as the basic structural unit of the *Testament*. (Even before the fifteenth century, the *huitain* was widely used by Guillaume de Machaut and other poets who worked with the genre of the *ballade*.) The octosyllabic verse, often written with a slight pause, or *césure*, after the first four syllables, is one of the oldest and most widely used verses in French poetry, dating back to the tenth century. The symmetry created by the balance between the octosyllabic verse and the eight-line strophe or *huitain* heightens the mirrorlike effects of the work, occasionally accentuated by verbal play and repetition within the huitain, such as the discourse of the abbot:

> De cecy neusse point envie
> Mais il convient le **pas passer**
> . . . .
> Se vous voulez bien tres**passer**
> On savise tard en mourant.

The mirror play of the text neatly complements that of the accompanying images, with the corpses reflecting the living figures, projecting their bodies into the advanced stage of deterioration that will eventually follow their death.

Didactic Implications

The moral thrust of the *danse macabre*, of course, extends beyond a simple contemplation of human mortality. The dance is strongly colored by religious overtones, especially those related to sin, contrition, and judgment. Josette Wisman contextualizes the *danse macabre* within an earlier iconographic tradition highlighting the theme of divine judgment:

---

[6] See M. Freeman, "The Dance of the Living: Beyond the Macabre in Fifteenth-Century France," in *Sur quel pied danser?: Danse et literature*, ed. E. Nye (Amsterdam: Rodopi, 2005), 11–30.

Le jugement dernier est évoqué à plusieurs reprises. Comme dans l'iconographie qui commence à apparaître dès le XIIIe siècle sur les tympans de nombreuses églises et cathédrales, on peut lire dans les danses des allusions à Dieu le juge, au compte qui est gardé de bonnes et mauvaises actions de chaque être humain et qui sont placées sur une balance et/ou inscrites dans un livre, le *liber vitae*. ("La symbolique," 161)

The dialogue between the living and the dead returns frequently, directly or obliquely, to the theme of judgment. Nor are caveats related to divine judgment limited to the secular participants in the dance. The bishop, confronted by the image of his own death, realizes that he is not ready to face his destiny: "Dieu vouldra de tout compte oir / Cest ce que plus me desconforte." [God wants to hear a complete accounting / This is what distresses me most.] Whether or not Jean Gerson (1363–1429), the famous Parisian theologian, is the author of the poem, as an early tradition claims, the work is clearly marked by strong didactic, even homiletic overtones. It has been conjectured that the *danse macabre* may have begun as a mimed accompaniment to a sermon on death and final judgment. The hortatory tone of the text is certainly unmistakable.

Proverbial Refrain

Every stanza of the *Danse Macabre* ends with a proverb, recasting or reinforcing the message of the speaker. The practice of incorporating proverbs into a poetic text, especially as the last verse of a stanza, enjoyed great popularity among fifteenth-century French poets, such as Michault Taillevent, Pierre Chastellain, Jean Molinet, Guillaume Coquillart, and most notably François Villon. The rhetorical function of the proverb, both in the *Danse Macabre* and in its many manifestations prevalent throughout fifteenth-century French poetry, is to generate a voice of authority.[7] The proverbial conclusion to each *huitain* of the *Danse Macabre* enriches the tonality of the work by adding another voice, complementing the voices of the living and the dead that sustain the extended dialogue, validating the message of the text by linking it to popular wisdom.

Many of the proverbs remind the reader of the inevitability and finality of death. The king, at the end of his speech, observes, "En la fin fault devenir cendre" ("In the end, all become ash"), a thought echoed by the knight's closing proverb, "Dessoubz le ciel na rien estable" ("There is nothing lasting under heaven"), by the squire, "Tous fault morir on ne scet quant" ("We all must die, no

---

[7] Useful are J. Morawski, *Proverbes français* (Paris: Champion, 1925); J.W. Hassell, *Middle French Proverbs* (Toronto: PIMS, 1982); and E. Schulze-Busacker, *Proverbes et expressions proverbiales dans la littérature narrative du Moyen Âge français* (Paris: Champion, 1985).

one knows when"), and by other figures in the work. In contrast to this type of proverb with its stoic acceptance of death, there is another type, characterized by an ironic edge and a mocking perspective on human ambition. These proverbial twists issue from the dead more often than from the living. The corpse-partner of the abbot tells him, "Le plus gras est premier pourry" ("The fattest one is the first to rot"), and the king's skeletal partner ends his speech with an ironic commentary on the futility of material wealth, "Le plus riche na qun linceul" ("The richest man's only possession is a shroud").

In addition to their popularity among French poets of the fifteenth century, proverbs were frequently incorporated into sermons of the period, and collections of proverbs, both in Latin and in the vernacular, were available as a resource to preachers. Some of these proverbs are based on biblical texts, while others have been collected from popular sources. As early as the thirteenth century, theologians such as Jacques de Vitry were urging preachers to incorporate proverbs into their homilies, especially those destined for a lay audience. The didactic aspect of these proverbs made them especially useful as a complement to certain arguments expounded in medieval homilies. In addition to the authority of biblical teachings, Church Fathers, and theologians, these arguments could also be supported with an appeal to collective experience, popular wisdom, and common sense, all exemplified in the proverb. Furthermore, the proverb retains a certain plasticity, molding itself to the context in which it appears, with its application and interpretation dependent upon its immediate context. Given the highly didactic nature of the *Danse Macabre* with its strong homiletic overtones, and the widely diverse popular audience to which it is directed, the proverb proves a very appropriate and effective literary device for the purposes of the poet.

Image and Text

A full and accurate understanding of the *danse macabre*, at least in the form of Guyot Marchant's book, cannot be achieved without some appreciation of the interplay between images and text. J. H. M. Taylor, in an article entitled "Danse Macabré and Bande Dessinée: A Question of Reading," explains how the two representations of the dance interrelate:

> . . . the Dance places itself at that moment of equilibrium between life and death. Now I submit that this reading of the Dance—which is important for a proper understanding of the message (there is still—just—time for an act of contrition) is not easily achievable either from the text alone, or from the image alone. The concatenation of text and image is an indispensable tool for the moralist. (365–66)

It is not known whether the image or the text was created first. A possible clue, however, may be found in the portion of the text concerning the bishop. The corpse opens his discourse:

> Tantost naures vaillant ce pic
> Des biens du monde et de nature
> Evesque de vous il est pic
> Non ostant vostre prelature

[Soon all your worldly and natural wealth / Will not be worth even this pick / Bishop, you are finished / Notwithstanding your bishopric.]

Although the corpses depicted in the panels occasionally carry an implement (a pick, a shovel, a spear), this is the only reference in the poem to an object carried by a death figure. While the pick is part of a pattern of implements reflected in other panels, and thus appears indigenous to the visual depiction of the *danse macabre*, the textual reference has no parallel in the poem, and thus stands out as an isolated example. I would argue that it seems far more likely that the text focuses here on an aspect of a pre-existing visual image, than the reverse. It is easy to imagine that the corpse's pick (which, like the shovel, suggests the grave about to be dug) caught the poet's eye, and that he decided to work it into the text as a pretense for a rather clumsy pun, which occurs in the next two verses: *Evesque de vous il est pic / Non ostant vostre prelature*. It is much more difficult, I would contend, to imagine the reverse, i.e., that the artist seized on an isolated and seemingly random feature of the poem as a pretense to introduce an important artistic motif into the series of panels. Furthermore, the demonstrative adjective, *ce pic*, seems to strongly suggest that the poet is referring to a visible object.

Two passages from the end of the poem also suggest the primacy of the image over the text. The dead king, the last character other than the author to speak in the poem, urges the audience to heed the warning of the *danse macabre*: (boldface added for emphasis)

> Vous qui en ceste *portraiture*
> *Veez* danser estas divers,
> Pensez que humainne nature
> Ce nest fors que viande a vers.

[All you who **see** in this **painting** / Men of all conditions joining in the dance / Know that human existence / Is no more than meat for worms.]

The gaze of the spectator is again suggested in the conclusion of the author, immediately following the dead king's discourse:

Chascun le voit par ceste danse
Pour ce vous qui veez listoire
Retenez la bien en memoire.

[As everyone can see in this dance / Therefore, you who see this painting /
Remember it well.]

The word *istoire*, especially in conjunction with the verb *veez*, can be reasonably
translated as "painting" (a definition listed in Greimas, *Dictionnaire du moyen
français*). All of this evidence, then, appears to support the conclusion that the
image predates the text. Nevertheless, the question remains open to debate in the
absence of more conclusive evidence.

One could argue that there are actually two distinct discourses present in
Guyot Marchant's version of the *danse macabre*: the didactic voice of the text with
its strong homiletic overtones, and the farcical body language of the dancing
corpses. At one level, each page maintains the illusion of a symbiotic relationship between image and text, each somehow expanding, illustrating, commenting on the other. At another level, however, the relationship is one of opposition
rather than synthesis. The eye is naturally drawn to the graphic representation
of the scene before settling on the verbal version of the confrontation. There is
little doubt that the encounter with death is rendered far more powerfully and
dramatically in the former than the latter. The text, then, is essentially relegated
to a purely secondary role, a mere corollary of the iconography, reduced in effect
to the role of a gloss, an exegetical elaboration on the primary representation of
the drama. The opposition between the graphic and the textual renditions of
the *danse macabre* may be taken as the reflection of the conflict between the two
modes of discourse present in the book—one associated with the Church, incarnated in the figure of the *Acteur*, the other associated with the theater, incarnated
in the corpse figures, which appear in various ludic postures.[8]

Guyot Marchant

We know relatively little about Guyot Marchant. He maintained an active printing practice in Paris in the last two decades of the fifteenth century, often publishing six to nine books in a year, and sometimes as many as thirteen to fifteen.
The majority of his publications were scholarly works in Latin, mostly in the
range of thirty-six to forty leaves. Sandra Hindman highlights the academic ori-
entation of Marchant's books:

    [8] See S. Oosterwijk, "Money, Morality, Mortality: The Migration of the *Danse
Macabre* from Murals to Misericords," in *Freedom of Movement in the Middle Ages*, ed. P.
Horden (Donington: Shaun Tyas, 2007), 37–56.

From the large number of theological and humanist works published by Marchant, we can surmise that he aimed most of his works at a university clientele. (. . .) This same circle of hypothetical readers from the schools would have been interested in the newest writings by the latest thinkers, letters by Erasmus and Pico della Mirandola, and treatises by Lefèvre d'Etaple, the Parisian pre-Reformation humanist, most of whose works were published in Paris by Marchant. ("The Career," 80)

In addition to the Latin treatises, Marchant occasionally published works in the vernacular, notably the *Danse Macabre* (the edition of 1485 followed by the expanded edition of 1486, and eventually the *Grand danse macabre des femmes* in 1491) and the *Calendrier des bergers* (1493), an encyclopedic collection including medicine, astrology, astronomy, and theology. These works were destined for a less elite clientele. According to an inventory of sixteenth-century Parisian libraries (Hindman, "The Career," 90), twice as many copies of the 1485 edition of the *Danse Macabre* ended up in the hands of bourgeois families as aristocratic families. Clearly, this book, like the *Calendrier des bergers*, was marketed for a popular audience, and, judging by the sequels to the original edition of the *Danse Macabre*, it seems that the work sold quite well. Hindman presents this general characterization of Marchant as a printer:

> Having successfully identified this [academic and theological] market, he made a number of astute business decisions: he was careful to restrict his press runs so that his editions sold out, and to sell his books through more than one outlet. He typically included sparse pictorial adornments in his editions so as to enhance their appeal . . . But the "popular" books for which he is best known, the Dance and the Calendar, are anomalous in his career. ("The Career," 93)

The degree to which the woodcuts of Marchant's edition accurately reproduce the images on the walls of the Parisian cemetery is uncertain. On one hand, it has been established that the creator of the woodcuts has taken at least minor liberties with the original images, partially modernizing the style of dress and shoes, for example. On the other hand, it seems inconsistent that Guyot Marchant, who obviously intended to reproduce the *danse macabre* in a portable form that would eventually spread its fame well beyond the confines of Paris, would take the trouble of accurately reproducing the poem appearing on the cemetery walls, but would content himself with only a poor likeness of the fresco images, especially knowing that Parisian buyers of the book, the immediate audience for whom it was presumably intended, would inevitably compare the woodcuts to the original. In the absence of any authenticated copy of the frescoes from the Innocents, any claim that the reproductions are totally accurate simply cannot be solidly substantiated. It does seem plausible, however, to assume that Marchant's illustrations probably represent a reasonable likeness of the original images.

Encouraged by the success of his first edition of the *Danse Macabre*, Marchant published a collection of thematically related works concerning death: an expanded version of the *Danse Macabre* (adding a number of new figures including the duke, the schoolmaster, the pilgrim, the shepherd, and the jailer); a *Danse des femmes*, clearly a spinoff from the male version of the dance with a text written by Martial d'Auvergne; a version of the *Dit des trois morts et trois vifs*; and a series of shorter thematically related pieces concerning death and mortality. These works, in various combinations, were republished by Marchant through the remainder of the fifteenth century, with the *Danse Macabre*, in its expanded version, claiming the most numerous editions. Versions of this book, published by local printers in other cities, began appearing within a few decades in Geneva, Lyon, Rouen, and Troyes.

1485 Edition of *Danse Macabre*

Only one copy of the 1485 edition has survived, held by the Bibliothèque Municipale de Grenoble.[9] Several pages are missing from the front of the book, but the absent material can be reconstructed from the convergence of several reliable sources: first, two manuscripts in the Bibliothèque nationale, both of which were written shortly after the appearance of the *danse macabre* frescoes and poem in 1424, in which the scribe claims to have faithfully reproduced the verses found on the walls of the Parisian cemetery; and, second, the English translation of the poem, written by John Lydgate during a stay in Paris in 1426, just two years after the *danse macabre* mural and the accompanying inscription had been completed.[10]

> Like the example whiche that at Parise
> I fownde depicte ones on a walle . . .
> I toke on me to translaten al
> Owte of the frensshe Macabrees daunce.
> (*The Dance of Death*, p. 2, 19–20; p. 4, 23–24)

Lydgate's translation ended up under the frescoes of the *danse macabre* painted on the cloister walls of St. Paul's Cathedral in London in the 1430s, inspired by the mural in Paris. It is very likely that while John Lydgate was studying the images and inscription that he found on the interior walls of the Innocents, others were

---

[9] A facsimile of this edition was published in 1969: Pierre Vaillant, ed., *La Danse Macabre de 1485* (Grenoble: Editions des Quatre Seigneurs, 1969).

[10] The manuscripts in question are Paris, B.N., fonds français 25550 and fonds latin 14904.

engaged in similar contemplation, preparing to duplicate the *danse*, with varying degrees of fidelity, in other regions of France and western Europe.

The current translation is based on the facsimile of Marchant's 1485 edition, published by Pierre Vaillant (Conservateur en Chef de la Bibliothèque de Grenoble) in 1969. In reproducing the text, I have attempted to remain consistent with the principles established by Alfred Foulet and Mary Speer in *On Editing Old French Texts*, as well as those adopted by Ann Tukey Harrison in her excellent translation, *The* Danse Macabre *of Women*.

Subjects for Reflection

1. Does the author seem to treat some figures more sympathetically than others? Explain.
2. What conclusions, if any, may be drawn from such differentiated treatment?
3. If you were to establish such a hierarchy of occupations today, which professions/trades would you include, and how would you rank them?
4. Why do the Cleric and the Hermit come after the Child?
5. Who is going to Heaven and who to Hell? Which figures face an uncertain fate?
6. Why are there no notions of Heaven and Hell present in this work?
7. Which figures indicate regret and resistance, and which ones seem to accept their death more stoically?
8. Discuss some differences between the representation of death in the text and its representation in the accompanying images.
9. How might a fifteenth-century reader be affected differently by reading the text and by viewing the images?
10. What are the author's primary objectives? What kind of reaction and reflection is he trying to provoke from the reader?
11. What can be read from the body language of the figures in the woodcuts?
12. How do the figures of the dead mock the living?
13. Why does the author alternate secular and religious figures in descending order of importance? What aspects of late medieval social order are reflected in this dichotomy?
14. What is the importance of symbolic objects in the images? Provide a few examples of objects held by various figures, and explain their significance.
15. How do the images differ from the text in general tone? Do the images parallel the somber tone of the text, or do they occasionally show evidence of playfulness and humor? Explain.
16. Why are the figures of the dead presented in a state of partial deterioration rather than simple skeletons? What is the artist's intention?
17. Why are the lawyer and the musician placed very near the bottom of the social hierarchy?
18. Why does the work end with the figure of the dead king?
19. Is there a difference between the reaction of the religious figures and the secular figures when confronted by death? Are the religious figures, by virtue of their spiritual discipline, more accepting of death?
20. How do you explain the popularity of the *danse macabre* motif in the late medieval period?
21. Given the regrets expressed by the living figures, how would they live their lives differently if given another chance?
22. In the introductory verses we find: "In this mirror each person can read / How he will have to dance." In what senses is the work a mirror? How is the image of the mirror intensified by the location of the *danse macabre* in the Cemetery of the Innocents?
23. How was the effect of the original *danse macabre* altered when the large frescoes were reduced to small black-and-white woodcuts?
24. The work is characterized by its publisher as a *miroer salutaire pour toutes gens*. In what sense can the work be considered salutary rather than morbid?
25. Are there any contemporary works of art, fiction, or films that roughly parallel the *danse macabre*, forcing the readers/viewers to squarely confront their own mortality?

Danse Macabre

Lacteur

O creature raysonnable
Qui desires vie eternelle
Tu as cy doctrine notable
Pour bien finer vie mortelle
La dance macabre sappelle
Que chascun a danser apprant
A homme et femme est naturelle
Mort nespargne petit ne grant

En ce miroer chascun peut lire
Quil lui convient ainsi danser
Saige est celuy qui bien sy mire
Le mort le vif fait avancer
Tu vois les plus grans commancer
Car il nest nul que mort ne fiere
Cest piteuse chose y panser
Tout est forgie dune matiere

The Author

O creature of reason,
You who desire life eternal,
Behold a remarkable lesson
On how to finish your mortal life.
It is called the *danse macabre*,
Which teaches us all how to dance.
Such is the natural condition of man and
    woman,
Death spares neither the humble nor the great.

In this mirror each can read
That he will have to dance in this way.
Wise is he who observes himself in it cor-
    rectly.
The corpse makes the living one step forward.
You see those of highest station begin,
For Death spares no one.
It is a subject of sad reflection,
All men are made of the same matter.

Le Mort

Vous qui vivez certainnement
Quoy quil tarde ainsi danceres
Mais quant dieu le scet seulement
Advisez comme vous feres
Dam pape vous commenceres
Comme le plus digne seigneur
En ce point honore seres
Aux grans maistre est deu lonneur

The Corpse

You who live: certainly,
Sooner or later, you will do this dance.
But when? God alone knows.
Consider well how you will act.
Sir Pope, you will begin,
As he who holds the highest place,
Thus will you be honored.
To one of high station all honor is due.

Le Pape

He fault il que la dance mainne
Le premier qui suis dieu en terre
Jay eu dignite souverainne
En leglise comme saint pierre
Et comme autre mort me vient querre
Encore point morir ne cuidasse
Mais la mort a tous mainne guerre
Peu vault honneur que si tost passe

The Pope

Ah, is it I who must lead off the dance,
I who represent God on Earth?
I have had sovereign honor
In the Church, like Saint Peter,
And yet Death seeks me like any other.
I did not think myself ready to die,
But Death wages war on us all.
Of little worth is honor that perishes so
     quickly.

Le Mort

Et vous le non pareil du monde
Prince et seigneur grant emperiere
Laisser fault la pomme dor ronde
Armes ceptre timbre baniere
Je ne vous lairay pas derriere
Vous ne povez plus signorir
Jenmaine tout cest ma maniere.
Les filz adam fault tout mourir

The Corpse

And you, peerless one, Prince and Lord,
Great emperor of the world,
You must leave behind this round apple of
     gold,[1]
Arms, scepter, crown, banner.
I will not leave you behind;
You can no longer rule.
I lead away every man; this is how I work.
All the sons of Adam must die.

Lempereur

Je ne sçay devant qui japelle
De la mort quansi me demainne
Arme me fault de pic de pelle
Et dun linceul ce mest grant paine
Sur tous ay eu grandeur mondaine
Et morir me fault pour tout gage
Questce de mortel demainne
Les grans ne lont pas davantage

The Emperor

I do not know where to appeal,
Concerning Death who treats me thus.
I must arm myself with a pick, a shovel,
And a shroud; this grieves me greatly.
Over all I held worldly domain,
And death is my only payment.
What is the meaning of mortal dominion?
It confers no advantage on the powerful.

---

[1] Refers to the imperial orb or *Reichsapfel*, symbolizing universal rule.

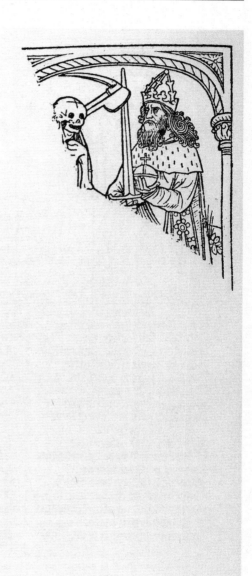

Le mort

Vous faictez lefbay fe femblé
Cardinal: fus legierement:
Suiuons les autres tous enféblé
Rien ny vault efbaiffement.
Vous auez vefcu haultement.
Et en honneur a grant deuis:
Prenez en gre lefbatement.
En grant honneur fe pert laduis

Le cardinal

Jay bien caufe de mefbair
Quant ie me voy de cy pres pris.
La mort meft venuee affallir:
Plus ne veftiray vert ne gris.
Chapeau rouge chappe de pris
Me fault laiffer a grant deftreffe:
Je ne lauoye pas apris.
Toute ioye fine en trifteffe.

Le mort

Venes noble roy couronne
Renomme de force et de proeffe:
Jadis fuftez enuironne
De grant pôpez: de grãt nobleffe
Mais maintenãt toute haultteffe
Laiffere: vous neftes pas feul.
Peu autres de voftre richeffe.
Le plus riche na qun lînceul.

Le roy

Je nay point apris a danfer
A danfe et note fi fauuage
Las: on pent voir et penfer
Que vault orgueil force lignage.
Mort deftruit tout: ceft fon vfage:
Auffi toft le grant que le maindre.
Qui moing fe prife plus eft fage.
En la fin fault deuenir cendre:

Le Mort

Vous faictez lesbay ce semble
Cardinal sus legierement
Suivons les autres tous ensemble
Rien ny vault ebaissement
Vous avez vescu haultement
Et en honneur a grant devis
Prenez en gre lesbatement
En grant honneur se pert ladvis

The Corpse

You seem astonished, it seems to me,
Cardinal, step lively,
Let's follow the others together:
Astonishment changes nothing.
You have lived a life of luxury
With honor and great distinction.
Enjoy the fun,
In great honor wisdom is lost.

Le Cardinal

Jay bien cause de mesbair
Quant je me voy de cy pres pris
La mort mest venuee assallir
Plus ne vestiray vert ne gris
Chapeau rouge chappe de pris
Me fault laisser a grant destresse
Je ne lavoye pas apris
Toute joye fine en tristesse

The Cardinal

Indeed I have cause to be astonished
When I see myself trapped.
Death has come to attack me,
I will no longer wear green or gray.
With great remorse I must abandon
My red hat, my fine cape.
I had never learned
That all joy finishes in sadness.

Le Mort

Venes noble roy couronne
Renomme de force et de proesse
Jadis fustez environne
De grant pompez de grant noblesse
Mais maintenant toute hautesse
Laisseres vous nestes pas seul
Peu aures de vostre richesse
Le plus riche na qun linceul

The Corpse

Come, noble crowned king,
Renowned for power and prowess.
You were once surrounded
By great pomp and nobility,
But now you will abandon
All majesty; you are not alone.
Your wealth will do you little good.
The richest man's only possession is a shroud.

Le Roy

Je nay point apris a danser
A danse et note si sauvage
Las on peut veoir et penser
Que vault orgueil force lignaige.
Mort destruit tout cest son usage
Aussi tost le grant que le maindre
Qui moing se prise plus est sage
En la fin fault devenir cendre

The King

I never learned to dance
To such a fierce tune and step.
Alas, one can see and weigh
The true worth of pride, power, lineage.
Death destroys all, it is his custom,
The powerful as quickly as the weakest.
He who values himself least is wise:
In the end, all become ash.

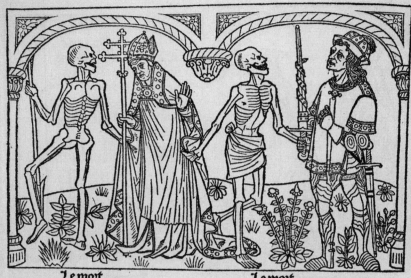

Le mort

Patriarche pour basse chiere
Vous ne pouez estre quitte
Vostre double croix quaues chiere
Vng autre aura: cest equite.
Ne pensez plus a dignite.
Ja ne seres pape de romme
Pour rendre compte estes cite
Fole esperance decoit lome

Le patriarche

Bien apercoy que mondain honeur
Ma deceu: pour dire le voir
Mes ioyes tornent en doleur.
Et que vault tant donneur auoir.
Trop hault monter nest pas sauoir
Haulx estas gastet gens sans nobre
Mais peu le veulent parcevoir.
A hault monter le fais encombre

Le mort

Cest de mon droit que ie vous mainne
A la danse gent connestable:
Les plus fors come charlemaigne
Mort prent cest chose veritable:
Rien ne vault chere espouentable
Ne forte armeure en cest assault
Dun cop iabatz le plus estable.
Rien nest darmes quat mort assault

Le connestable

Jauoye encor entencion
Dassaillir chasteaulx forteresses.
Et mener a sugection
En aquerant honneurs richesses.
Mais ie voy que toutes proesses
Mort met au bas: cest grat despit
Tout luy e vng: doulceurs rudesses
Contre la mort na nul respit.

Le Mort

Patriarche pour basse chiere
Vous ne povez estre quitte
Vostre double croix quaves chiere
Ung autre aura cest equite
Ne pensez plus a dignite
Ja ne seres pape de romme
Pour rendre compte estes cite
Folle esperance decoit lomme

The Corpse

Patriarch, your throne
Will not free you from this fate.
Your double cross that you so cherish
Will go to another; this is only just.
Do not dwell any longer on glory,
You will never be Pope of Rome.
You are called upon to account for yourself,
Foolish hope deceives many a man.

Le Patriarche

Bien apercoy que mondain honneur
Ma deceu, pour dire le voir
Mes joyes tornent en doleur
Et que vault tant donneur avoir
Trop hault monter nest pas savoir
Haulx estas gastent gens sans nombre
Mais peu le veulent parcevoir
A hault monter le fais encombre

The Patriarch[2]

I realize that worldly honor
Has deceived me, to tell the truth.
My joy has turned to sorrow,
And what is the value of so much honor?
To climb too high is not a sign of wisdom.
High stations ruin people without number,
But few are willing to realize it.
The summit encumbers those who climb
    too far.

Le Mort

Cest de mon droit que je vous mainne
A la danse gent connestable
Les plus fors comme charlemaigne
Mort prent cest chose veritable.
Rien ne vault chiere espoventable
Ne fortes armeure en cest assault
Dun cop jabatz le plus estable
Rien nest darmes quant mort assault

The Corpse

It is my right to lead you away
To the dance, noble constable.
Even the most powerful, like Charlemagne,
Are seized by death; this is the very truth.
A terrifying countenance will do you no good,
Nor strong weapons against this assault:
With one blow I cut down the firmest
    opponent.
Weapons are useless when Death attacks.

Le connestable

Javoye encor entencion
Dassaillir chateaulx forteresses
Et mener a sugection
En aquerant honneurs richesses
Mais je voy que toutes proesses
Mort met au bas cest grant despit
Tout luy est ung doulceurs rudesses
Contre la mort na nul respit

The Constable[3]

I still intended
To attack castles and strongholds,
And subjugate the enemy
Acquiring honor and wealth.
But I see that Death brings down
All power: this is great insult.
Everything is the same to him, gentleness
    or violence.
Against death there is no respite.

---

[2] A bishop who holds the highest episcopal rank after the pope.
[3] The commander of all royal military forces.

Le mort

Que vous tires la teste arriere
Archeuesque: tirez vous pres.
Auez vous peur qnon ne voꝰ fiere
Ne doubtez: vous venres apres.
Nest pas tousiours la mort epres
Tout hôme: et le suit coste a coste.
Rendre conuient debtes et prest.
Une foys fault compter a loste

Larcheuesque

Las: ie ne scay ou regarder
Tât suis par mort a grant destroit
On fuiray ie pour moy aider.
Certes qui bien la congnoistroit
Hors de raison iamais nistroit.
Plus ne gerray en châbre painte.
Morir me conuient cest le droit.
Quât faire fault cest grât côtraite.

Le mort

Vous qui entre les grans barons
Aues eu renon cheuallier:
Obliez trompettes clarons
Et me suiuez sans sommellier.
Les dames solies reueillier
En faisant danser longue piece.
A autre danse fault veillier.
Ce que lun fait lautre despiece.

Le cheualier

Or ay ie este auctorise
En pluseurs fais: et bien fame.
Des grans et des petis prise:
Auec ce des dames ame.
Ne oncques ne fus diffame
A la court de seigneur notable:
Mais a ce cop suis tout pasme.
Dessoubz le ciel na rien estable.

Le Mort

Que vous tires la teste arriere
Archevesque tirez vous pres
Avez vous peur quon ne vous fiere
Ne doubtez vous venres apres
Nest pas tousjours la mort enpres
Tout homme et le suit coste a coste
Rendre convient debtes et prestz
Une foys fault compter a loste

Larchevesque

Las je ne sçay ou regarder
Tant suis par mort a grant destroit
Ou fuiray je pour moy aider
Certes qui bien la congnoistroit
Hors de raison jamais nistroit
Plus ne gerray en chambre painte
Morir me convient cest le droit
Quant faire fault cest grant contrainte

Le Mort

Vous qui entre les grans barons
Aves eu renon chevallier
Obliez trompettes clarons
Et me suivez sans sommellier
Les dames solies reveillier
En faisant danser longue piece
A autre danse fault veillier
Ce que lun fait lautre despiece

Le Chavalier

Or ay je este auctorise
En pluseurs fais et bien fame
Des grans et des petis prise
Avec ce des dames ame
Ne oncques ne fus diffame
A la court de seigneur notable
Mais a ce cop suis tout pasme
Dessoubz le ciel na rien estable

The Corpse

Why do you draw your head back,
Archbishop? Come close.
Are you afraid you will be struck?
Do not fear: you will come next:
Is not Death always near
Every man, following along, side by side?
It is time to pay up your debts;
In the end the host must be paid.

The Archbishop

Alas, I do not know where to look,
I am so closely pressed by Death,
Where shall I flee to find refuge?
Surely anyone who knew Death well
Would never stray from reason.
I will no longer lie in a painted room,
It is fitting that I die, it is only right.
When the time comes, there is great distress.

The Corpse

You who among the great barons
Have enjoyed great renown, Sir Knight,
Forget trumpets, clarions,
And follow me without your packhorse.
You used to regale the ladies
With tireless dancing;
It is time to give attention to another dance,
What one builds, another destroys.

The Knight

I have been truly blessed with good fortune
In many deeds, and widely acclaimed,
Admired by both the noble and the humble
And, moreover, loved by women.
I was never disgraced
In the court of a worthy nobleman.
But with this blow I am completely lifeless.
There is nothing lasting under heaven.

Le mort

Tantoſt naures vaillant ce pic
Des biens du mõde et de nature
Eueſque: de vous il eſt pic
Non oſtant voſtre prelature.
Voſtre fait giet en auenture.
De vous ſubges fault rẽdre cõpte:
A chaſcun dieu fera droiture.
Neſt pas aſſeur q̃ trop hault mõte

Leueſque

Le ceur ne me peul eſtoir
Des nouuelles que mort maporte.
Dieu vouldra de tout compte oir:
Ceſt ce que plus me deſconforte.
Le monde auſi: peu me conforte:
Qui tous a la fin deſherite.
Il retient tout: nul rien nemporte.
Tout ce paſſe fors le merite.

Le mort

Auancez vous gent eſcuier
Qui ſaues de danſer les tours.
Lance porties: et eſcu hier:
Et huy vous fineres vos iours
Il neſt rien qui ne praigne cours.
Danſez: et panſez de ſuir.
Vous ne pouez auoir ſecours.
Il neſt qui mort puiſſe fuir.

Leſcuier

Puis que mort me tient en ſes las
Au mois que ie puiſſe vng mot dire
Adieu deduis: adieu ſolas:
Adieu dames: plus ne puis rire.
Penſez de lame qui deſire
Repos, ne vous chaille plus tant
Du corps: que tᵒˢ leſiours empire.
Tous fault morir on ne ſcet quant

Le Mort
Tantost naures vaillant ce pic
Des biens du monde et de nature
Evesque de vous il est pic
Non ostant vostre prelature
Vostre fait giet en aventure
De vos subges fault rendre compte
A chascun dieu fera droicture
Nest pas asseur qui trop hault monte

Levesque
Le cueur ne me peult esioir
Des nouvelles que mort maporte
Dieu vouldra de tout compte oir
Cest ce que plus me desconforte
Le monde aussi peu me conforte
Qui tous a la fin desherite
Il retient tout nul rien nemporte
Tout ce passe fors le merite

Le Mort
Avancez vous gent escuier
Qui saves de danser les tours
Lance porties et escu hier
Et huy vous fineres vos jours
Il nest rien qui ne praigne cours
Dansez et pansez de fuir
Vous ne povez avoir secours
Il nest qui mort puisse fuir

Lescuier
Puis que mort me tient en ses las
Aumoins que je puisse un mot dire
Adieu deduis adieu solas
Adieu dames plus ne puis rire
Pensez de lame qui desire
Repos ne vous chaille plus tant
Du corps que tous les jours empire
Tous fault morir on ne scet quant

The Corpse
Soon all your worldly and natural wealth
Will not be worth even this pick,
Bishop. You are finished,
Notwithstanding your bishopric.
Your destiny lies uncertain.
You must account for those in your charge:
God will deal justly with each man.
He is not safe who climbs too high.

The Bishop
My heart cannot rejoice
From the news that Death brings me.
God wants to hear a complete accounting,
This is what distresses me most.
This world, which in the end disinherits
    us all,
Offers me little consolation.
It [the world] keeps all things, I carry noth-
    ing away.
Everything vanishes except one's true
    worth.

The Corpse
Come forward, noble squire,
You who know so many dance steps.
You carried a lance and shield yesterday,
And today you will finish your days.
There is nothing that does not flow away.
Go ahead and dance, try to escape.
You will have no help.
There is no one who can flee death.

The Squire
Since Death holds me in his net,
At least let me say a word.
Farewell pleasure, farewell good fun,
Farewell ladies, I can no longer laugh.
Think of the soul that desires
Rest. Pay no more heed to the body
That declines with every day.
We all must die, no one knows when.

Le mort

Abbe: venez tost: vous fuyez:
Nayez ia la chiere esbaye
Il couient que la mort suyez,
Combien que moult lauez haye.
Commandez adieu labbaye:
Que gros et gras vous a nourry.
Tost pourrirez a peu de aye.
Le plus gras est premier pourry.

Labbe

De cecy nensse point ennse:
Mais il couient le pas passer.
Las: or nay ie pas en ma vie
Garde mon ordre sans casser.
Garde vous de trop embrasser
Vous qui viuez au demorant
Se vous voulez bien trespasser.
On sauise tart en mourant.

Le mort

Bailly qui sauez quest iustice:
Et hault et bas: en mainte guise
Pour gouuerner toute police.
Venez tantost a ceste assise.
Je vous adiourne de main mise
Pour rendre compte de vos fais
Au grant iuge: qui tout vng prise.
Vn chascun portera son fais.

Le bailly

Hee dieu: vecy dure iournee:
De ce cop pas ne me gardoye.
Or est la chance bien tournee:
Entre iuges honneur auoye.
Et mort fait raualer ma ioye:
Qui ma adiourne sans rappel.
Je ny voy plus ne tour ne voye:
Contre la mort na point dappel.

Le Mort

Abbe venez tost vous fuyez
Nayez ja la chiere esbaye
Il convient que la mort suyvez
Combien que moult lavez haye
Commandez a dieu labbaye
Que gros et gras vous a nourry
Tost pourrirez a peu de aye
Le plus gras est premier pourry

Labbe

De cecy neusse point envie
Mais il convient le pas passer
Las or nayje pas en ma vie
Garde mon ordre sans casser
Garde vous de trop embrasser
Vous qui vivez au demorant
Se vous voulez bien trespasser
On savise tard en mourant

Le Mort

Bailly qui savez quest justice
Et hault et bas en mainte guise
Pour gouverner toute police
Venez tantost a ceste assise
Je vous adjourne de main mise
Pour rendre compte de vos fais
Au grant juge qui tout ung prise
Un chascun portera son fais

Le Bailly

Hee dieu vecy dure journee
De ce cop pas ne me gardoye
Or est la chance bien tornee
Entre juges honneur avoye
Et mort fait ravaler ma joye
Qui ma adjourne sans rappel
Je ny voy plus ne tour ne voye
Contre la mort na point dappel

The Corpse

Abbot, come quickly, you who flee.
Do not wear such an astonished countenance,
It is only fitting that you follow Death,
Although you have hated him greatly.
Commend to God your abbey
Which has nourished you so well.
You will decay within a short time:
The fattest one is the first to rot.

The Abbot

I haven't the least desire for this,
But the step must be taken.
Alas, did I not during my life
Keep my vows without fail?
Be careful not to embrace too much,
You who remain among the living,
If you want to die well.
It's too late to change your mind when you die.

The Corpse

Bailiff, you who know about justice,
High and low and in many forms,
In order to enforce all laws,
Come immediately to this court.
I summon you by force
To render account of your deeds
To the great judge who judges us all.
Each one will bear his burden.

The Bailiff

Oh God, this is a painful day.
I was not expecting this blow,
Now my fortune has turned:
I used to be honored among judges,
And Death, who has sentenced me without
    recourse,
Has forced me to swallow my joy.
I see no way out.
Against death there is no appeal.

Le mort

Maistre: pour vostre regarder
En hault: ne pour vostre clergie:
Ne pouez la mort retarder.
Cy ne vault rien astrologie.
Toute la genealogie
Dadam qui fut le premier homme
Mort prent: ce dit theologie.
Tous fault morir pour vne pomme.

Le maistre

Pour science: ne pour degrez:
Ne puis auoir prouision
Car maintenant tous mes regrez
Sont: morir a confusion.
Pour finable conclusion
Je ne scay rien que plus descrine.
Je pers cy toute aduision.
Qui vouldra bien morir: bien viue

Le mort

Bourgois: hastez vous sas tarder.
Vous nauez auoir ne richesse
Qui vous puisse de mort garder.
Se des biens dont eustes largesse
Aues bien vse: cest sagesse
Dautruy viet tout a autruy passe
Fol est qui damaser se blesse.
On ne scet pour qui on amasse.

Le bourgois

Grant mal me fait: si tost laissier
Rentes: maisons: cens: nourritures
Mais poures: riches: abaissier
Tu faiz mort: telle est ta nature.
Sage nest pas la creature
Damer trop les biens qu demeure
Au monde: et sot siens de droiture.
Ceulx q plus ont: plus enuiz meuret.

Le Mort

Maistre pour vostre regarder
En hault ne pour vostre clergie
Ne povez la mort retarder
Cy ne vault rien astrologie
Toute la genealogie
Dadam qui fut le premier homme
Mort prent ce dit theologie
Tous fault mourir pour une pomme

The Corpse

Master, neither your gazing at the heavens,
Nor all your knowledge,
Can delay the arrival of Death.
Astrology is powerless here.
All the descendants of Adam,
Who was the first man,
Are claimed by death, theology tells us.
We all must die because of one apple.

Le Maistre

Pour science ne pour degrez
Ne puis avoir provision
Car maintenant tous mes regrez
Sont morir a confusion
Pour finable conclusion
Je ne sçay rien que plus descrive
Je pers cy toute advision
Qui vouldra bien morir, bien vive

The Astrologer

Neither my knowledge nor my academic
   degrees
Furnish me resources [to escape].
For now I deeply regret
Dying in defeat
At the very end of my life.
I don't know anything else to write,
I've lost all power to interpret dreams.
Let him who wants to die well, live well.

Le Mort

Bourgeois hastez vous sans tarder
Vous navez avoir ne richesse
Qui vous puisse de mort garder
Se des biens dont eustes largesse
Aves bien use cest sagesse
Dautruy vient tout a autruy passe
Fol est qui damasser se blesse
On ne scet pour qui on amasse

The Corpse

Bourgeois, hasten without delay.
You have neither wealth nor riches
That can save you from Death.
If you put your abundant wealth
To good use, you have acted wisely.
Everything comes from another, and goes
   to another.
It is folly to build a fortune at great personal
   cost.
One never knows for whom one is collect-
   ing wealth.

Le Bourgeois

Grant mal me fait si tost laissier
Rentes maisons cens norritures
Mais pouvres riches abaissier
Tu faiz mort telle est ta nature
Sage nest pas la creature
Damer trop les biens qui demeurent
Au monde et sont siens de droiture
Ceulx qui plus ont plus enuiz meurent

The Bourgeois

It pains me so to part so soon
With investments, houses, income, food.
But both the poor and the rich
You cut down, Death; such is your nature.
Foolish is the creature
Who is too attached to wealth
That remains in the world, where it prop-
   erly belongs.
Those who have the most die with the most
   regret.

Le mort

Sire chanoine prebendez:
Plus ne aures diſtribucion:
Ne gros: ne vous y attandez:
Prenez cy conſolacion.
Pour toute retribucion
Morir vous conuient ſãs demeure
Ja ny aurez dilacion.
La mort viẽt quon ne garde leure.

Le chanoine

Cecy gueres ne me conforte:
Prebendez fus en mainte egliſe.
Or eſt la mort plus que moy forte:
Qui tout emmainne ceſt ſa guiſe.
Blanc ſeurplis et amuſſe griſe
Me faut laiſſier: et a mort rendre.
Que vault gloire ſy tout bas miſe.
A bien mourir doit chaſcun tendre.

Le mort

Marchant: regerdez par deca:
Pluſeurs pais aues cerchie
A pie: a cheual: de pieca:
Vous nen ſeres plus empeſchie.
Vecy voſtre dernier merchie.
Il conuient que par cy paſſez.
De tout ſoing ſeres deſpechie.
Tel couuoite qui a aſſez.

Le marchant

Jay eſte amont et aual:
Pour marchander ou ie pottoye.
Par long temps apie: acheual:
Mais maintenãt pers toute ioye.
De tout mon pouoir acqueroye:
Or ay ie aſſez mort me contraint.
Bon fait aler moyenne voye.
Qui trop embraſſe peu eſtraint.

Le Mort

Sire chanoine prebendez
Plus ne aures distribucion
Ne gros ne vous y actendez
Prenez cy consolacion
Pour toute retribucion
Mourir vous convient sans demeure
Ja ny aurez dilacion
La mort vient quon ne garde leure

The Corpse

Sir Canon, possessing a prebend,
You will no longer collect your contributions,
Or small coins; nor should you expect it.
Take consolation here.
As your only reward,
You must die without delay:
You will have no reprieve.
Death comes when you're not looking at the
  clock.

Le Chanoine

Cecy gueres ne me conforte
Prebendez fus en mainte eglise
Or est la mort plus que moy forte
Que tout emmainne cest sa guise
Blanc seurpelis et amusse grise
Me fault laissier et a mort rendre
Que vault gloire sy tost bas mise
A bien mourir doit chascun tendre

The Canon

This hardly brings me comfort.
I possessed a prebend in many churches,
Now Death is stronger than I,
Death who carries everyone away: this is
  his custom.
The white surplice and the gray cassock
I must leave behind and abandon to Death.
Of what worth is a glory so easily brought
  down?
We must all strive to die well.

Le Mort

Marchant regardez par deça
Pluseurs pays aves cerchie
A pie et a chevalz de pieça
Vous nen seres plus empeschie
Vecy vostre dernier merchie
Il convient que par cy passez
De tout soing seres despechie
Tel convoite qui a assez

The Corpse

Merchant, look over here.
You have traveled through many countries,
On foot and on horseback for a long time.
You will no longer be burdened.
This is your last transaction,
You have to go through with this.
You will be relieved of all cares.
He who has enough desires more.

Le Marchant

Jay este amont et aval
Pour marchander ou je povoye
Par long temps apie acheval
Mais maintenant pers toute joye
De tout mon povoir acqueroye
Or ay je assez mort me contraint
Bon fait aler moyenne voye
Qui trop embrasse peu estrain

The Merchant

I have been upstream and downstream
To trade where I could,
Long have I traveled on foot and on horse-
  back.
But now all my pleasure is lost.
I devoted all my attention to collecting wealth;
Now I have enough; Death is closing in.
It is good to take the middle road:
He who embraces too much grasps little.

Le mort

Alez marchant sans plus rester:
Ne faites ia cy resistence.
Vous ny poues rien conquester.
    Vous aussi homme dastinence
Chartreux: prenez en pacience.
De plus viure nayes memoire.
Faittes vous valoir a la dance.
Sur tout homme mort a victoire

Le chartreux

Ie suis au monde pieca mort:
Par quoy de viure ay moins enuie
Ia soit que tout hôme craint mort.
Puis que la char est assouuie:
Plaise a dieu que lame rauie
Soit es cielx apres mon trespas.
Cest tout neant de ceste vie.
Tel est huy: qui demain nest pas.

Le mort

Sergent qui portez celle mace:
Il semble que vous rebellez.
Pour neant faittez la grimace:
Se on vous greue si appellez.
Vous estez de mort appellez.
Qui luy rebelle il se decoit.
Les plus fors sont tost rauallez.
Il nest fort quausi fort ne soit.

Le sergent

Moy qui suis royal officier:
Comme ose la mort frapper.
Ie fasoie mon office hier:
Et elle me vient huy happer.
Ie ne scay quel part eschapper:
Ie suis pris: deca et dela.
Malgre moy me laisse apper.
Enuiz meurt qui apris ne la.

Le Mort

Allez marchant sans plus rester
Ne faites ja cy resistence
Vous ny poves rien conquester
Vous aussi homme dastinence
Chartreux prenes en pacience
De plus vivre nayez memoire
Faictez vous valoir a la dance
Sur tout homme mort a victoire

The Corpse

Off with you, merchant:
Leave without resistance:
There's no profit for you here.
You also, man of abstinence,
Carthusian friar, take all things with
    patience.
Relinquish all memory of life,
Acquit yourself well in the dance.
Death has victory over every man.

Le Chartreux

Je suis au monde pieça mort
Par quoy de vivre ay moins envie
Ja soit que tout homme craint mort
Puis que la char est assouvie
Plaise a dieu que lame ravie
Soit es ciel apres mon trespas
Cest tout neant de cette vie
Tel est huy qui demain nest pas

The Carthusian Friar

I have long been dead to this world,
And thus have less desire to live,
Although all men fear death.
Since the flesh is satisfied,
May it please God that my transported soul
Find itself in Heaven after my death.
This life is worth nothing at all:
What is here today is gone tomorrow.

Le Mort

Sergent qui portez cette mace
Il semble que vous rebellez
Pour neant faictez la grimace
Se on vous greve si appellez
Vous etez de mort appellez
Qui luy rebelle il se deçoit
Les plus forts sont tost ravallez
Il nest fort quausi fort ne soit

The Corpse

Officer of the peace, you who carry this mace,
You appear to be resisting.
It does no good to grimace,
And to cry out if threatened.
You are summoned by Death,
He who resists deceives himself.
The strongest ones are quickly swallowed up,
As strong as a man may be, there is always
    one stronger.

Le Sergent

Moy qui suis royal officier,
Comme mose la mort frapper
Je fasoye mon office hier
Et elle me vient huy happer
Je ne sçay quelle part eschapper
Je suis pris deça et dela
Malgre moy me laisse apper
Enuiz meurt qui appris ne la

The Officer of the Law

I who am a royal officer,
How dare Death strike me?
Yesterday I was doing my duty,
And today he comes to snatch me away.
I cannot find a way to escape,
I am trapped, no matter where I go.
Despite my efforts, I find myself seized.
He who hasn't learned this truth dies today.

Le mort

Ha maistre: par la passeres
Nayez ia soig de vous deffedre
Plus hômes nespoventeres.
Aprez moinne sãs plus actêdre
Ou pésez vous: cy fault entêdre
Tâtost aurez la bouche close
Vôme nest: fors que vêt et cêdre
Vie dôme est moult peu de chose.

Le moinne

Jamasse mieux encore estre
En cloistre et faire mon seruice
Cest vng lieu deuot et bel estre
Or ay ie comme fol et nice
Ou têps passe cômis mait vice
De quoy nay pas fait penitâce
Souffisant. dieu me soit propice
Chascun nest pas ioyeux ĝ dãse.

Le mort

Usurier. de sens desreugle
Venez tost: et me regardez
Dusure estes tant aueugle
Que dargêt gaigner tout ardez.
Mais vous en serez bien lardez
Car se dieu qui est merueilleux
Ma pitie de vous: tout perdez
A tout perdre: est cop perilleux.

Lusurier

De conuient il si tost mozir:
Ce mest grât pase ẽ grât greuã
Et ne me pourroit secourir.   ce
Mon oz: mô argêt: ma cheuãce
Je voys mozir: la mort mauãce
Mail il men desplait sôme toute
Quest ce de male acoustumance:
Tel a beaux yeux ĝ ne voit goute.

Le poure hôme

Usure est tant
maluaiz pechie
Comme chascun
dit: et raconte.
Et cest homme:
qui approuchie
Se set de la mozt:
nen tient conte.
Mesme largent:
quê ma mai côpte
Encore a vsure
me prette.
Il deura de re
tour au compte.
Nest pas quitte:
qui doit de reste.

Le Mort

Ha maistre par la passeres
Naiez ja soing de vous deffendre
Plus hommes nespoventeres
Apres moine sans plus actendre
Ou pensez vous cy fault entendre
Tantost aurez la bouche close
Homme nest fors que vent et cendre
Vie domme est moult peu de chose

The Corpse

Ah, Master, you will go this way,
Make no effort to save yourself.
You will frighten men no longer.
You're next, monk, without delay,
What are you thinking of? You must
    understand.
Soon your mouth will be sealed.
A man is nothing but wind and ash,
A man's life has scarcely any worth.

Le Moinne
Jamasse mieulx encore estre
En cloistre et faire mon service
Cest ung lieu devost et bel estre
Or ay je comme fol et nice
Au temps passe commis maint vice
De quoy nay pas fait penitance
Souffisant dieu me soit propice
Chascun nest pas joyeux qui danse

Le Mort
Usurier de sens desreugles
Venez tost et me regardez
Dusure estes tant aveugles
Que dargent gaignez tout ardez
Mais vous en seres bien lardez
Car se dieu qui est merveilleux
Na pitie de vous tout perdez
A tout perdre est cop perilleux

Lusurier
Me convient il si tost morir
Ce mest grant peine et grevance
Et ne me pourroit secourir
Mon or mon argent ma chevance
Je vois morir la mort mavance
Mais il men desplait somme toute
Quest ce de male acoustumance
Tel a beaux yeux qui ne voit goute

Le Povre Homme
Usure est tant maulvaiz pechie
Comme chascun dit et raconte
Et cest homme qui approuchie
Se sent de la mort nen tient conte
Mesme largent quen ma main compte
Encore a usure me preste
Il devra de retour au compte
Nest pas quitte qui doit de reste

The Monk
I would prefer to still be
In the cloister singing Mass,
It's a devout place and a good life.
Like a foolish and stupid man,
I have, in the past, committed many sins,
For which I haven't sufficiently repented.
May God be merciful to me,
All who dance are not joyful.

The Corpse
Usurer, having lost all sense of moderation,
Come quickly and look at me.
You are so blinded by usury
That you burn with greed for money,
But you will be wounded by your avarice,
For if God, who is wondrous,
Does not take pity on you, you will lose all
  you have,
And to lose everything is a perilous blow.

The Usurer
Must I die so soon?
This grieves and pains me greatly,
And neither my gold, my silver, nor any of
  my wealth
Can possibly save me.
I am going to die, Death advances toward me,
Even though I may not like it.
What is the reason for this evil custom?
Some who have sharp eyes don't see a thing.

The Poor Man
Usury is indeed an evil sin
As anyone will tell you,
And yet this man who feels Death
  approaching
Fails to realize it.
Even now he counts his money into my hand
To be repaid with interest.
He will have to settle his own account:
One who owes is not free of debt.

Le mort

Medecin a tout voſtre orinne
Voies vous icy quamander:
Jadis ſceuſtes de medecinne
Aſſes pour pouoir commander.
Or vous vient la mort demander.
Côme autre vous conuient mozir:
Vous ny poues contremander.
Bon mire eſt qui ſe ſcet guerir.

Le medecin

Long têps a quê lart de phiſique
Jay mis toute mon eſtudie.
Jauoye ſcience: et pratique.
Pour guerir maintes maladie.
Je ne ſcay que ie contredie
Plus ny vault herbe ne racine:
Nautre remede quoy quon die.
Contre la mort na medicine.

Le mort

Gentil amozeux gent et frique
Qui vous cuidiez de grant valeur:
Vous eſtes pris la mort voº pique.
Le monde lares a douleur.
Trop lauez ame: ceſt foleur:
Et a mozir peu regarder.
Ja toſt vous changeres coleur.
Beaute neſt quymage farder.

Lamozeux

Helas: oz ny a il ſecours
Contre mort adieu amourettes:
Moult toſt va ieuneſſe a decours.
A dieu chapeaux bouquez fleuretes
A dieu amans: et puceletes:
Souienne vous de moy ſouuent.
Et vous mirez ſe ſages eſtes:
Petite pluie abat grant vent.

Le Mort

Medecin a tout vostre orinne
Voies vous icy quamander
Jadis sceutes de medicine
Asses pour povoir commander
Or vous vient la mort demander
Comme autre vous convient morir
Vous ny poves contremander
Bon mire est qui se scet guerir

Le Medicin

Long temps a quen lart de phisique
Jay mis toute mon estudie
Javoye science et pratique
Pour guerir mainte maladie
Je ne sçay que je contredie
Plus ny vault herbe ne racine
Nautre remede quoy quon die
Contre la mort na medecine

Le Mort

Gentil amoreux gent et frique
Qui vous cuidez de grant valeur
Vous estes pris la mort vous pique
Le monde lares a doleur
Trop lavez ame cest foleur
Et a morir peu regarder
Ja tost vos changeres coleur
Beaute nest quymage farder

Lamoreux

Helas or ny a il secours
Contre mort adieu amourettes
Moult tost va jeunesse a decours
A dieu chapeaux bouques fleuretes
A dieu amans et pucelettes
Souvienne vous de moy souvent
Et vous mirez se sages estes
Petite pluie abat grant vent

The Corpse

Physician, with your reading of urine,
Do you see any remedy here?
You once knew enough about medicine
To order cures,
Now Death comes to claim you.
Like any other, you must die.
You cannot order any remedy against it.
It is a good doctor who can cure himself.

The Physician

I have devoted long years
To the study of medicine.
I had the knowledge and the experience
To cure many a sickness.
I do not know what to prescribe,
All herbs and roots are powerless,
As is any other remedy that one may
    propose:
Against death there is no medicine.

The Corpse

Noble lover, gracious and handsome,
Who think yourself so grand,
You are finished; Death strikes you down.
You will abandon this world in sorrow.
You have loved it too much, sheer folly,
And you have given little thought to dying.
Soon you will lose your color,
Beauty is nothing but a tinted statue.

The Lover

Alas, is there no rescue
From death? Farewell love affairs.
Youth flows quickly away.
Farewell hats, bouquets, little flowers,
Farewell lovers and maidens,
Remember me often,
And look deeply into yourselves if you are wise:
A gentle rain calms a mighty wind.

Le mort
Passes cure sans plus songier:
Je sens questez abandonne.
Le vifz le mort solies mengier:
Mais vous seres aux vers done.
Vous fustez iadis ordonne
Miroer dautruy: et exemplaire.
De vous fais seres guerdonne.
A toute painne est deu salaire.

Le cure
Veille ou non il fault que me rende
Il nest homme que mort nassaille.
Heer de mes parroissiens offrende
Nauray iamais: ne funeraille.
Deuant le iuge fault que ie aille.
Rendre compte: las doloreux:
Or ay ie grant peur que nefaille.
Qui dieu quitte bien est eureux.

Le mort
Laboreur qui en soing et painne
Auez vescu tout vostre temps:
Morir fault cest chose certainne
Reculler ny vault: ne contens.
De mort deues estre contens:
Car de grant soucy vous deliure.
Approuchiez vous ie voz attens
Folz est qui cuide tousiour viure.

Le laboureur
La mort ay souhaite souuent
Mais volentier ie la fuisse:
Jamasse mielx fist pluye ou vent
Estre es vignes ou ie fouisse:
Encor plus grant plaisir y prisse
Car ie pers de peur tout propos.
Or nest il qui de ce pas ysse.
Au monde na point de repos.

Le Mort

Passes cure sans plus songer
Je sens questez abandonne
Le vif le mort solies menger
Mais vous seres aux vers donne
Vous fustez jadis ordonne
Miroer dautruy et exemplaire
De vos fais seres guirdonne
A toute painne est deu salaire

The Corpse

You go next, parish priest; don't give it a
    thought:
I see that you are on your own.
You used to earn your bread from the living
    and the dead,
But you will now be given over to the worms.
You were once ordained
To serve as a model and example for others,
You will be rewarded for your deeds:
Every hardship has its compensation.

Le Cure

Veille ou non il fault que me rende
Il nest homme que mort nassaille
He de mes parroisiens offrende
Nauray jamais ne funeraille.
Devant le juge fault que je aille
Rendre compte las doloreus
Or ay je grant peur que ne faille
Qui dieu quitte bien est eureux

The Parish Priest

Whether I want to or not, I must surrender,
Death spares no man.
I will never have another donation
From my parishioners, nor funeral offering.
I must go before the judge
To account for myself, alas, wretch that I am.
Now I greatly fear that I will fail:
Happy is he whom God acquits.

Le Mort

Laboreur qui en soing et painne
Avez vescu tout vostre temps
Morir fault cest chose certainne
Reculier ny vault ne contens
De mort deves estre contens
Car de grant soussy vous delivre
Approchiez vous je vous actens
Folz est qui cuide tousjour vivre

The Corpse

Plowman, you who have spent
All your life in hardship and toil,
You must die, this is for certain,
There is no use in trying to escape or argue.
You ought to be happy with Death,
For he frees you from a heavy burden.
Come close, I'm waiting for you.
He is mad who believes he will live forever.

Le Laboureur

La mort ay souhaite souvent
Mais volentier je la fuisse
Jamaisse mielx fit pluye ou vent
Estre es vignes ou je fouisse
Encore plus grant plaisir y prisse
Car je pers de peur tout propos
Or nest il qui de ce pas ysse
Au monde na point de repos

The Plowman

I have often wished for Death,
But I willingly flee it.
I prefer, whether in rain or wind,
To be plowing in the vineyard,
I take even greater pleasure there,
For I lose all sense of fear.
Is there not anyone who can escape this fate?
In this world there is no rest.

Le mort

Aduocat fans long proces faire
venez voftre caule plaidier.
Bien auez fceu les gens attraire
De pieca: non pas duy ne dier.
Confeil: cy ne vous peult aidier.
Au grant iuge vous fault venir:
Sauoir le deues fans cuidier.
Bon fait iuftice preuenir.

Laduocat

Ceft bien droit que raifon fe face
Ne ie ny fcay mectre deffence:
Contre mort na refpit ne grace:
Nul napelle de fa fentance.
Jay eu de lautruy quant ie y pêce
De quoy ie doulte eftre repris.
A craindre eft le iour de vengence.
Dieu rendra tout a iufte pris.

Le mort

Meneftrel qui danfes et notes
Sauez: et anez beau maintien
Pour faire eftouir fos et fotes:
Suen dictez vous allós nous bien
Môftrer voˀ fault puis que voˀ tiê
Aux autres cy: vng tour de danfe
Le contredire ny vault rien.
Maiftre doit monftrer fa fciêce

Le meneftrel

De danfer ainfy neuffe cure
Certes trefenuiz ie men meffe:
Car de mort neft painne plus dure
Jay mis foubz le banc ma vielle.
Plus ne corneray fauterelle
Ne autre danfe: mort men retient
Il me fault obeir a elle.
Tel danfe a qui au ceur nen tient

Le Mort

Advocat sans long proces faire
Venez vostre cause plaidier
Bien aves sceu les gens actraire
De pieça non pas duy ne dier
Conseil si ne vous peut aidier
Au grant juge vous fault venir
Savoir le deves sans cuidier
Bon fait justice prevenir

Ladvocat

Cest bien droit que raison se face
Ne je ny sçay mectre deffence
Contre mort na respit ne grace
Nul napelle de sa sentence
Jai eu de lautruy quant je y pence
De quoy je doubte estre repris
A craindre est le jour de vengence
Dieu rendra tout a juste pris

Le Mort

Menestrel qui danses et notes
Savez et avez beau maintient
Pour faire esjoir sos et sotes
Quen dictez vous allons nous bien
Monstrer vous fault puis que vous tien
Aux autres cy ung tour de danse
Le contredire ny vault rien
Maistre doit monstrer la science

Le Menestral

De danser ainsi neusse cure
Certes tres ennuiz je men mesle
Car de mort nest painne plus dure
Jay mis soubz le banc ma vielle
Plus ne corneray sauterelle
Nautre danse mort men retient
Il me fault obeir a elle
Tel danse a qui au cueur nen tient

The Corpse

Lawyer, without making a long case,
Come plead your cause.
You have long been able to impress people,
Not just today or yesterday.
No counsel can help you now.
You must appear before the great judge.
Know this with certainty,
A good deed prevents harsh punishment.

The Lawyer

It is only right that justice be done,
Nor can I construct a valid defense.
Against Death there is no reprieve or delay,
No one appeals his sentence.
I've behaved toward others, now that I
    reflect on it,
In a manner deserving of blame.
The day of vengeance is to be feared:
God will give each one just what he deserves.

The Corpse

Musician, you who know how to dance
And write music, and whose pleasing ways
Amuse foolish men and women,
What do you say? Are we doing well?
Since you are now within my grasp,
Teach the others a new dance step.
It will do you no good to refuse,
The master must demonstrate his art.

The Musician

I would not care to dance like this.
Surely I take part with great reluctance
For there is no harsher pain than death.
I've put my fiddle beneath the bench,
I'll never play another jig
Or any other dance; Death forbids it.
I must obey him,
Some dance even though their heart isn't in it.

Le mort

Faictes voye: vous aues tort
Laboureur. Apres cordelier
Souuent aues preschie de mort
Si vous deues mois merueillier.
Ja ne sen fault esmay baillier.
Il nest si fort que mort narrefte.
Si fait bon a morir veillier.
A toute heure la mort est preste

Le cordelier

Quest ce: que de biure en ce monde
Nul homme a seurte ny demeure
Toute vanite y habonde
Puis diet la mort q̃ to⁹ court sure
Mendicite point ne matture:
Des meffais fault paier lamende
En petite heure dieu labeure.
Sage est le pecheur qui samende

Le mort

Petit enfant na gueres net
Au monde auras peu de plaisance
A la danse seras mene
Côme autres, car mort a puissâce
Seur tous: du iour de la naissance
Conuient chascun a mort offrir:
Fol est qui nen a congnoissance.
Qui plus vit plus a a souffrir

Lenfant

A. a. a. ie ne scay parler
Enfant suis: iay la langue mue.
Hier nasquis huy men fault aler
Je ne faiz quentree et yssue
Rien nay meffait. mais de peur sue
Prêdre ê gre me fault cest le mieulx
Lordonnance dieu ne se mue.
Aussi tost meurt ieusne que vieulx

Le Mort

Faictes voye vous avez tort
Laboureur Apres cordelier
Souvent aves preschie de mort
Si vous devez moins merveillier
Ja ne sen fault esmay ballier
Il nest si fort que mort nareste
Si fait bon a morir veillier
A toute heure la mort est preste

Le Cordelier

Quest ce que de vivre en ce monde
Nul homme a seurte ny demeure
Toute vanite y habonde
Puis vient la mort qua tous court sure
Mendicite point ne massure
Des mesfais fault paier lamende
En petite heure dieu labeure
Sage est le pecheur qui samende

Le Mort

Petit enfant na guere ne
Au monde auras peu de plaisance
A la danse seras mene
Comme autre car mort a puissance
Seur tous du jour de la naissance
Convient chascun a mort offrir
Fol est qui nen a congnoissance
Qui plus vit plus a a souffrir

Lenfant

A a a je ne sçay parler
Enfant suis jay la langue mue
Hier nasquis huy men fault aller
Je ne faiz quentree et yssue
Rien nay mesfait mais de peur sue
Prendre en gre me fault cest le mieulx
Lordonnance dieu ne se mue
Ainsi tost meurt jeune que vieux

The Corpse

Move along; you are wrong,
Plowman. Next, mendicant friar,
You have often preached about death,
So you ought not be surprised,
You should not be the least bit astonished.
Even the strongest men are stopped by Death.
One should therefore reflect on dying,
For Death is ready at every moment.

The Mendicant Friar

What does it mean to live in this world?
No man resides safely here.
The world abounds in vanity,
Since Death ruins all in the end.
A life of begging offers me no protection,
The price of misdeeds must be paid.
God works in short time,
Wise is the sinner who repents.

The Corpse

Little child, barely born,
You will have little pleasure in this world.
You will be led to the dance
Like any other, for Death has dominion
Over all. From the day of his birth
Everyone must offer himself to Death:
Whoever does not realize this is a fool.
The more one lives, the more one will suffer.

The Child

Ah, ah, ah, I don't know how to speak:
I am a child, my tongue is mute,
I was born yesterday, today I must leave,
All I do is enter and exit.
I have done no wrong, but I sweat with fear;
It is best that I willingly accept
The rule. God does not change his mind.
The young die as quickly as the old.

Le mort

Cuidez voz de mort eschapper
Clerc esperdu pour reculer:
Il ne sen fault ia defripper.
Tel cuide souuent hault aler
Quon voit acop tost raualler.
Prenez en gre: alons enseble
Car rien ny vault le rebeller.
Dieu punit tout qt bo luy seble

Le clerc

Fault il qun ieusne clerc seruat
Qui en seruice prent plesir
Pour cuider venir en auant
Meure il tost: cest desplaisir.
Je suis quitte de plus choisir
Autre estat, il fault quasi dase,
La mort ma pris a son loisir.
Moult remaist de ce que fol pese

Le mort

Clerc: point ne fault faire refus
De danser: faicte vous valoir.
Vous nestes pas seul: leues sus:
Pour tat mois voz edoit chaloir
Venes apres cest mon voloir
Homme nourry en hermitage:
Ia ne vous en couient douloir.
Vie nest pas seur heritage

Le hermite

Pour vie dure ou solitaire
Mort ne donne de viure espace.
Chascun le voit: si sen fault taire
Or reger dieu qun don me face
Cest que tous mes pechies efface
Bien suis cotens de tous ses biés
Desquelx iay vse de sa grace.
Qui na souffisance il na riens

Le mort

Cest bien dit:
ainsi doit on dire.
Il nest qui soit
de mort deliure.
Qui mal vit
il aura du pire.
Si pense chun
de bien viure.
Dieu pesera
tout a la liure
Bon y fait peser
soir et main:
Meilleur science
na en liure.
Il nest qui ait
poit de demain

Le Mort

Cuidez vous de mort eschapper
Clerc esperdu pour reculer
Il ne sen fault ja defripper
Tel cuide souvent hault aler
Quon voit acop tost ravaller
Prenez en gre alons ensemble
Car rien ny vault le rebeller
Dieu punit tout quant bon lui semble

The Corpse

Do you think you can escape Death,
Confused cleric, by sneaking away?
One can never flee.
He who believes he has ascended
Is often seen to suddenly tumble.
Accept your fate, let's go together,
For it is useless to resist.
God punishes everyone as he sees fit.

Le Clerc

Fault il qun jeusne cler servant
Qui en service prent plesir
Pour cuider venir en avant
Meure si tost cest desplesir
Je suis quitte de plus choisir
Altre estat il faut quansi danse
La mort ma pris a son loisir
Moult remaint de ce que fol pense

Le Mort

Clerc point ne fault faire refus
De danser faicte vous valoir
Vous nestes pas seul leves sus
Pour tant mois voz en doit chaloir
Venez apres cest mon voloir
Homme nourry en hermitage
Ja ne vous en convient doloir
Vie nest pas seur heritage

Le Hermite

Pour vie dure ou solitaire
Mort ne donne de vivre espace
Chascun le voit si sen fault taire
Or requier dieu qun don me face
Cest que tous mes pechies efface
Bien suis contens de tous ses biens
Desquelx jay use de sa grace
Qui na souffisance il na riens

Le Mort

Cest bien dit ainsi doit on dire
Il nest qui soit de mort delivre
Qui mal vit il aura du pire
Si pense chacun de bien vivre
Dieu pesera tout a la livre
Bon y fait penser soir et main
Meilleur science na en livre
Il nest qui ait point de demain

The Cleric

Must it be that a young cleric in active service,
Who takes pleasure in serving
Because he believes he will advance,
Should die so soon? This is a bitter loss.
I am spared the choice
Of a higher position. Thus I must dance,
Death has taken me at his whim.
Much remains of a fool's thoughts.

The Corpse

Cleric, you must not refuse
To dance: acquit yourself well.
You are not alone, rise up,
Do not let this vex you so.
Come along next, this is my will,
You who spent your life in a hermitage.
It will do you no good to grieve,
Life is not inherited property.

The Hermit

In exchange for a hard and solitary life
Death does not extend one's time.
This is plain to see, and we must keep silent.
Now I pray God that He allow me one gift,
That He efface all my sins.
I am content with all the blessings
That I have been given by His grace.
Whoever does not have contentment, has
  nothing.

The Corpse

This is well said, thus should one speak.
There is no one delivered from Death,
Whoever lives badly will have even worse,
So let each of us think about living well.
God will weigh everything by the pound,
It is right to reflect on this, both day and
  night.
No better knowledge will be found in any
  book,
There is no one who has no tomorrow.

Mortales dominus cikos in luce creauit: Ut capiant meritis
gaudia summa poli. Felix ille quid qui mentem ingiter illoc
Dirigit: atq̃ vigil nopia quoq̃ cauet. Nec tamen infelix./sce
leris quem penitet acti: Quicq̃ suum facinus plãgere sepe solet
Sed viuãt vana fouet: Quicq̃ mors nulla sequatur: Et velut inter
nos fabula vana foret. Cum doceat sensus viuentes morte re
solui: Atq̃ hered/ penas pagina sacra probet.   Quos qui no.
meruit infelix pxoxius et amene Ciuit. et extinctus sentiet ille/
rogum. Sic igitur cuncti sapientes viuere certent: Ut nichil
inferni sit metuenda palus.

Ung roy mort

Vous: qui en ceste pourtraicture
Veez danser estas diuers.
Pensez quest humainne nature
Ce nest fors que viande a vers.
Je le monstre: qui gis enuers:
Si ay ie este roy coronnez.
Telz seres vous: bons: et peruers.
Tous estas: sont aux vers dõnes.

        Lacteur

Rien nest dõme: qui bien y pense.
Cest tout vent: chose transitoire.
Chascun le voit: par ceste danse.
Pour ce: vous qui veez listoire
Retenez la bien en memoire.
Car hõmes et fẽmes elle amoneste:
Dauoir de paradis la gloire.
Eureux est: qui es cielx fait feste.

Mais aucuns sont a qui nenchault
Comme sil ne fust paradis:
Ne enfer. helas: il auront chault.
Les liures que firent iadis
Les sains: le mõstrẽt en beaux dis.
Acquitez vous qui cy passes:
Et faictez des biens: plus nen dis.
Bien fait vault moult es trespasses

Cy finist la dãse macabre imprimee
par vng nomme guy marchant de
morant au grãt hostel du college de
nauarre en champ gaillart aparis
Le vinthuitisime iour de septembre
Mil quatre cẽt quatre vingz et cinq

Un Roy Mort

Vous qui en ceste portraiture
Veez danser estas divers
Pensez que humainne nature
Ce nest fors que viande a vers
Je le montre qui gis envers
Si ay je este roy couronnez
Tels seres vous bons et pervers
Tous estas sont a vers donnes

Lacteur

Rien nest homme qui bien y pense
Cest tout vent chose transitoire
Chascun le voit par ceste danse
Pour ce vous qui veez listoire
Retenez la bien en memoire
Car homme et femme elle amoneste
Davoir de paradis la gloire
Eureux est qui es cieulx fait feste

Mais aucuns sont a qui nen chault
Comme sil ne fut paradis
Ne enfer helas il auront chault
Les livres que firent jadis
Les sains le monstrent en beaux dis
Acquitez vous que cy passes
Et faitez des biens plus nen dis
Bienfait valt moult es trespasses

Cy finit la danse macabre imprimee par ung nomme guy marchant demorant au grant hostel du college de navarre en champ gaillart a Paris le vinthuitieme jour de septembre mil quatre cent quatre vingz et cinq

A Dead King

All you who see in this painting
Men of all conditions joining in the dance,
Know that human existence
Is no more than meat for worms.
I, who lie here, show it clearly,
And I was once a crowned king.
So will you be, whether men of virtue or sin.
All stations of life end up with the worms.

The Author

All things considered, man is nothing,
He is only wind, a transitory thing,
As everyone can see in this dance.
Therefore, you who see this painting,
Remember it well,
For it urges all men and women
To strive for the glory of Paradise.
Happy are those who rejoice in Heaven.

But some pay no heed,
As if Heaven and Hell did not exist.
Alas, they will soon be warm.
The books written by the saints
Express this in beautiful words.
Commit yourselves, you who pass by here,
And do good; I'll say no more.
A good deed is greatly valued by the dead.

Here ends the *danse macabre* printed by a certain Guy Marchant residing in the College of Navarre, Champ Gaillart, in Paris, the twenty-eighth day of September, 1485.

Transcription and Translation of Latin Inscription

(Prepared by Professor Hugh Parker, Dept. of Classical Studies,
University of North Carolina at Greensboro)

Mortales Dominus cunctos in luce creavit:
 Ut capiant meritis gaudia summa poli.
Felix ille quidem qui mentem iugiter illuc
 dirigit: atque vigil noxia queque cavet.
Nec tamen infelix sceleris quem penitet acti
 quique suum facinus plangere sepe solet
Sed vivunt homines tanquam mors nulla sequatur:
 Et velut infernus fabula vana foret.
Cum doceat sensus viventes morte resolui:
 Atque herebi penas pagina sacra probet.
Quas qui non metuit infelix prorsus et amens
 vivit: et extinctus sentiet ille rogum
Sic igitur cuncti sapientes vivere certent:
 Ut nichil inferni sit metuenda palus.

The Lord has created all mortals in light so that they might grasp through their merits the highest joys of heaven. Indeed, he is continually happy who directs his mind in that direction, and the watchful person keeps clear of all harmful things. By the same token he is not unhappy who repents of a sin that was committed, and he who often is accustomed to lament his sin. But people live as if no death follows, and as if hell were an unreal myth, although sense teaches that the living are set free by death and sacred scripture proves the punishments of hell. He who has not feared these [the punishments] at all and lives foolishly will also upon his death feel the pyre. And so all wise people strive to live in such a way that the morass of hell should not be feared.

Bibliography

Appleford, A. "The Dance of Death in London: John Carpenter, John Lydgate, and the Daunce of Poulys." *Journal of Medieval and Early Modern Studies* 38 (2008): 285–314.

Ariès, P. *L'Homme devant la mort.* Paris: Editions du Seuil, 1977. *The Hour of Our Death.* New York: Knopf, 1981.

Baron, F. "Le médecin, le prince, les prélats et la mort: L'apparition du transi dans la sculpture française du Moyen Age." *Cahiers Archéologiques* 51 (2006): 125–58.

Batany, J. "Une image en négatif du fonctionnalisme social: les Danses Macabré." In *Dies Illa: Death in the Middle Ages*, ed. J.H.M. Taylor, 15–27. Liverpool: Francis Cairns, 1984.

Beaune, C., ed. *Journal d'un bourgeois de Paris: de 1405 à 1449.* Paris: Livre de Poche, 1990.

Binski, P. *Medieval Death: Ritual and Representation.* Ithaca: Cornell University Press, 1996.

Boase, T.S.R. *Death in the Middle Ages: Mortality, Judgment, and Remembrance.* London: Thames and Hudson, 1972.

Champion, P., ed. *La Danse Macabre de Guy Marchant.* Paris: Editions des Quatre Chemins, 1925.

Chaney, E.F., ed. *La Danse Macabré des Charniers des Saints Innocents à Paris.* Manchester: University of Manchester Press, 1945.

Clark, J.M. *The Dance of Death in the Middle Ages and the Renaissance.* Glasgow: Glasgow University Publications, 1950.

Cohen, J. "Death and the Danse Macabre." *History Today* 32 (August 1982): 35–40.

Cohen, K. *Metamorphosis of a Death Symbol: The Transi Tomb in the Late Middle Ages and the Renaissance.* Berkeley: University of California Press, 1973.

Corvisier, A. "La représentation de la societé dans les danses des morts du XVe au XVIIIe siècle." *Revue d'histoire moderne et contemporaine* 16 (1969): 489–539.

Couzy, H. "L'Eglise des Saints-Innocents à Paris." *Bulletin Monumental* 130 (1972): 279–302.

DeGirolami-Cheney, L., ed. *The Symbol of Vanitas in the Arts, Literature, and Music.* Lewiston, NY: Mellen, 1992.

Donzet, A.-J. "Les danses macabres." *Monuments Historiques* 124 (1982–1983): 49–52.

DuBruck, E. *The Theme of Death in French Poetry of the Middle Ages and the Renaissance*. Brussels: Mouton, 1964.

Duchâteau, V. *La danse macabre de la Chaise-Dieu*. St Ouen: La Goélette, 2006.

Dujakovic, M. "The Dance of Death, the Dance of Life: Cemetery of the Innocents and the Danse Macabre." In *Out of the Stream: Studies in Medieval and Renaissance Mural Painting*, ed. L.U. Afonso and V. Serrão, 206–32. Newcastle upon Tyne: Cambridge Scholars Publishing, 2007.

Espinosa, A. "Music and the *Danse Macabre*: A Survey." In *The Symbolism of Vanitas in the Arts, Literature, and Music*, ed. de Girolami-Cheney, 15–31. Lewiston, NY: Mellen, 1992.

Fein, D.A. "Guyot Merchant's Danse Macabre: The Relationship between Image and Text." *Mirator* 1 (August 2000): 1–11.

Finucane, R.C. "Sacred Corpse, Profane Carrion: Social Ideals and Death Rituals in the later Middle Ages." In *Mirrors of Mortality*, ed. J. Zhaley, 40–60. London: Europa, 1981.

Fleury, M., and G.-M. Leproux, eds. *Les Saints Innocents*. Paris: Délégation de l'Action Artistique de la Ville de Paris, 1990.

Foulet, A., and M.B. Steer. *On Editing Old French Texts*. Lawrence, KS: Regents Press of Kansas, 1979.

Freeman, M. "The Dance of the Living: Beyond the Macabre in Fifteenth-Century France." In *Sur quel pied danser?: Danse et littérature*, ed. E. Nye, 11–30. Amsterdam: Rodopi, 2005.

Gentry, F.G. *"Memento mori."* In *Oxford Dictionary of the Middle Ages* [*ODMA*], 3:1122. 4 vols. Oxford: Oxford University Press, 2010.

Gertsman, E. "Visual Space and the Practice of Viewing: The Dance of Death at Meslay-le-Grenet." *Religion and the Arts* 9 (2005): 1–37.

———. "Visualizing Death: Medieval Plagues and the Macabre." In *Piety and Plague: From Byzantium to the Baroque*, ed. F. Mormando and T. Worcester, 64–89. Kirksville, MO: Truman State University Press, 2007.

Greimas, A.J. *Dictionnaire du moyen français*. Paris: Larousse, 1992.

Groupe de Recherches sur les Peintures Murales, eds. *Vifs nous sommes. . . morts nous serons: La rencontre des trois morts et des trois vifs dans la peinture murale en France*. Vendôme: Editions du Cherche-Lune, 2001.

Gundersheimer, W.L. *The Dance of Death by Hans Holbein the Younger: A Complete Facsimile of the Original 1538 Edition of Les simulachres & historiees faces de la mort*. New York: Dover, 1971.

Harding, V. *The Dead and Living in Paris and London, 1500–1600*. Cambridge: Cambridge University Press, 2002.

Harrison, A.T. *The Danse Macabre of Women: Ms. fr. 995 of the Bibliothèque Nationale*. Kent, OH: Kent State University Press, 1994.

Hasenohr-Esnos, G., ed. *Le Respit de la mort par Jean le Fevre*. Paris: Société des Anciens Textes Français, 1969.

Hassell, J.W. *Middle French Proverbs, Sentences, and Proverbial Phrases*. Toronto: PIMS, 1982.

Hindman, S.L. "The Career of Guy Marchant (1483–1504): High Culture and Low Culture in Paris." In *Printing the Written Word: The Social History of Books, circa 1450–1520*, ed. eadem, 68–100. Ithaca and London: Cornell University Press, 1991.

Kinch, A. "The *Danse Macabre* and the Medieval Community of Death." *Mediaevalia* 23 (2002): 159–202.

Kowzam, J. "Dance of Death." In *ODMA*, 2:481.

Lydgate, J., F. Warren, and B.White. *The Dance of Death*. London: Published for the Early English Text Society by H. Milford, Oxford University Press, 1931.

Mâle, E. *L'Art religieux de la fin du Moyen Âge: étude sur l'iconographie du Moyen Âge et sur ses sources d'inspiration*. Paris: A. Colin, 1922.

Massip, F., and L. Kovàcs. "Les Franciscains et le genre macabre: les Danses de la Mort et la prédication." *European Medieval Drama* 8 (2004): 91–105.

McCullough, E. "The Dance of Death." *Journal of the Old Drogheda Society* 13 (2001): 23–26.

McGee, T.J. "Dances and Dance Music." In *ODMA*, 2:481–82.

Morawski, J. *Proverbes français antérieurs au XV⁰ siècle*. Paris: Champion, 1925.

Oosterwijk, S. *'Fro Paris to Inglond'? the Danse Macabre in Text and Image in Late-Medieval England*. Department of English Language and Culture, Faculty of Humanities, Leiden University, 2009.

———. "'I can but now, and now I go on my wai': The Presentation of the Infant in Medieval *danses macabres*." In *Essays on Medieval Childhood*, ed. J.T.Rosenthal, 124–50. Donington: Shaun Tyas, 2007.

———. "Of Corpses, Constables, and Kings: The *Danse Macabre* in Late Medieval and Renaissance Culture." *Journal of the British Archaeological Association* 157 (2004): 61–90.

———. "Of Dead Kings, Dukes and Constables: The Historical Context of the *Danse Macabre* in Later Medieval Paris." *Journal of the British Archaeological Association* 161 (2008), 131–62.

———. "Money, Morality, Mortality: The Migration of the *Danse Macabre* from Murals to Misericords." In *Freedom of Movement in the Middle Ages*, ed. P. Horden, 37–56. Donington: Shaun Tyas, 2007.

Oosterwijk, S., and Knoll, S., eds. *The Danse Macabre in Medieval and Early Modern Europe*. Newcastle upon Tyne: Cambridge Scholars Publishing, 2011.

Saugnieux, J. *Les danses macabres de France et d'Espagne et leurs prolongements littéraires*. Lyon: E. Vitte, 1972.

Schulze-Busacker, E. *Proverbes et expressions proverbiales dans la littérature narrative du Moyen Âge français*. Paris: Champion, 1985.

Spinrad, P.S. *The Summons of Death on the Medieval and Renaissance English Stage* Columbus, OH: Ohio State University Press, 1987.

Taylor, J.H.M., ed. *Dies Illa: Death in the Middle Ages*. Liverpool: Francis Cairns, 1984.

———. "*Danse Macabré* and *Bande Dessinée*: A Question of Reading." *Forum for Modern Language Studies* 25 (1989): 356–69.

———. "Poésie et prédication: La fonction du discours proverbial dans la Danse Macabre." *Medioevo Romanzo* 14 (1989): 215–26.

———. "Que signifiait danse au quinzième siècle? Danser la Danse macabre." *Fifteenth Century Studies* 18 (1991): 259–77.

———. "The Dialogues of the Dance of Death and the Limits of Late-Medieval Theatre." *Fifteenth-Century Studies* 16 (1990): 215–32.

Tenenti, A. *La vie et la mort à travers l'art du XVe siècle*. Paris: A. Colin, 1952.

Terrier, B. "Le Dict des trois morts et des trois vifs et sa représentation murale dans le centre de France." *Art Sacré* 14 (2001): 128–43.

Vaillant, P., ed. *La Danse Macabre de 1485, reproduite d'après l'exemplaire unique de la Bibliothèque de Grenoble et publiée sous l'égide de la Société des Bibliophiles Dauphinois*. Grenoble: Editions des Quatre Seigneurs, 1969.

———. "La danse macabre de 1485 et les fresques du charnier des Innocents (à Paris)." In *La Mort Au Moyen Âge*, 81–86. Strasbourg: Istra, 1977.

Wijsman, H. "La Danse macabre du cimetière des Saints-Innocents et un manuscrit de Philippe le Bon." In *Actes du 12ᵉ congrès international d'études sur les Danses macabres et l'art macabres en général*, 135–44. Meslay-le-Grenet: Association Danses Macabres d'Europe, 2003.

Wisman, J.A. "La symbolique du miroir dans les danses macabres de Guyot Marchant." *Romanische Forschungen* 103 (1991): 157–71.

———. "Un Miroir déformant: hommes et femmes des Danses Macabres de Guyot Marchant." *Journal of Medieval and Renaissance Studies* 23 (1993): 275–99.